MY LIFE AND TIMES WITH MYLES MUNROE

AN INSPIRATIONAL LIFE OF SERVICE

CHARLIE MASALA

MUNROE
PRESS

My Life and Times with Myles Munroe
©2022 Charlie Masala
ISBN: 978-0-620-92021-6
All rights reserved.

Published by Munroe Press
P.O. Box CB13070, Nassau, Bahamas
Email: office@munroeglobal.com
Website: www.munroeglobal.com

Editing
Andrew Cartwright, Outloud Media
Email: andrew@outloudmedia.co.za

Cover Design, Book Design, and Layout
Lesley Cartwright, Outloud Media
Email: lesley@outloudmedia.co.za

Cover Image: pexels.com, **Photos** of Dr. Myles Munroe used with permission.

Disclaimer
This publication is meant as a source of information for the reader. While every care has been taken to ensure accuracy, the author assumes no responsibility for errors, inaccuracies, omissions, or any other inconsistencies herein.

I am excited!

In your hand is the accumulated experiences of my lifetime with Dr Myles Munroe.

I hope that you will find this book educational, motivational, empowering and inspiring.

Yours to count on,

Charlie Masala

DEDICATION

To my beloved, departed Commanders-in-Chief, father, mother, mentor, and friends, **Dr. Myles E. Munroe** and **Mama Ruth Ann Munroe,** who led us with integrity, fearlessness, dedication, faithfulness, clarity, bravery, vision, valor, and victory!

To my beloved earthly father and mother, **Mushavhi-Mulungu-Ishe Ratshivhavho Wilson Masala (deceased)** and **Shandukani Jane (Johanna) Masala.** Through you, I received the gift of life. You instilled in me great values: hard work, patience, honor, respect, selflessness, and fairness.

CONTENTS

ACKNOWLEDGMENTS

First and foremost, my thanks to my beloved wife of nineteen years, **Xoli,** who has stood by me and encouraged me to do God's will for my life. To my children: **Zoe, Okona, and Andisa-Makaria-Ruth.** Thank you for allowing me to use my time, gifts, and talents to serve the world.

My biological parents, **Mushavhi Mulungu-Ishe Ratshivhavho Wilson Masala (late)** and **Mmawe Musoni Nwa-Buba Johanna Shandukani Masala,** for your great Kingdom parenting, life guidance, and grooming from childhood.

My sister, **Rudzani Masala,** who funded most of my higher education, and my other siblings—**Thomas Masala, Norman Masala, Linde Masala (late brother), Job Masala, and Una Masala-Rausina**—thank you for your encouragement over the years.

My spiritual parents, **Dr. T.S. Muligwe and Mma Rev. M.P. Muligwe,** for your spiritual guidance and grooming in the early days.

The Munroe family, **Dr. Myles & Mom Ruth Munroe.** You have been great mentors at an international level, exposing me to much of what life has to offer. I remain grateful. **Myles Munroe Jr. and Charisa Munroe-Wilborn,** for your continued support and belief in me in all the projects we have embarked on together, even after your parents' departure.

Dr. Basil Tryon & Ma Anne Tryon, for your unconditional love for me and my family. You have been a great financial supporter since you found that my life was devoted to the Kingdom and that I lived a life dedicated to serving Dr. Myles and Mama Ruth Munroe.

Pastor George Mosena and Mom Seny Mosena, for our relationship of thirty years and spiritual covering and encouragement in the twelve years at House of Faith.

My fellow members of the **Board of Trustees of the International Third World Leaders Association,** for your continued fellowship and support as my global family.

My College/Technikon friends: **Sizwe Sibeko, Happy Mabindisa, Thomas Madzivhe, Gideon Muvhumbe, Apostle Eddie Phetla, Sipho Maisela, Thandi Mulidzwi, and Mpho Khumalo** to name just a few, for encouraging me to lead and believing in my vision to invite Dr. Myles Munroe to be the speaker at our Technikon Northern Transvaal–Soshanguve campus in 1995.

In 1990, God used **Mr. Frederick and Mrs. Maria Neluheni** of Thohoyandou Block D to introduce me to the teachings of Myles Munroe. My friend, **Advocate Esau Ngwana,** and I used to visit their home frequently to enjoy a good meal and watch inspirational messages through their VHS video cassette player.

Pastor Edmund "Ed" Roebert and Auntie Pal Roebert, who partly sponsored me to take my first trip outside South Africa to visit my mentor Dr. Myles Munroe for the very first time in Nassau, Bahamas, in July 1997.

Dr. Dave Burrows and Ps. Angie Burrows, whom Dr. Myles assigned to be my hosts, as my visit coincided with the Youth Alive Conference that they led at the time. More importantly, for continuing the vision of my departed Commander-in-Chief, with excellence and diligence. The ministry has grown in his absence, which is a sign of great leadership as Dr. Myles taught that as a leader, "If what you build dies with you, you have been a failure."

Mr. Smith and Mrs. Rossi Smith, for accommodating me at your house and being great hosts during my first visit to Nassau, Bahamas, in July 1997.

Ms. Gail Vermeulen, for mentorship in my early days in Corporate South Africa.

Mr. Frans Saunders, through your life and coaching I became a better professional. You were not just my boss at African Bank but a brother, uncle, father, and knowledgeable mentor. Your sponsorship of my Global Leadership Summits in Nassau, Bahamas, made them one of the best and most educational experiences of my life.

My American brother, **Jerome Edmondson**, who helped me fight some of my diversity battles with white South African compatriots with racist tendencies.

My staff and team at **Myles Munroe International-Africa: Thabang Innocent Sadiki, Khanyi Gida, Rendani Makhokha (PA)**, and a team of administrators and volunteers I worked with over the years, including **Atabong Asong Gallows, Eugene Masebe Singo, Eugene Charnely,** and **Johannes Kurone.**

Mr. Terence Nkwashu, my former classmate and fellow believer groomed at TNT Student Christian Fellowship, for conducting the interviews in preparation for this book's material.

Eric and Mpumi Mabuza, for your friendship over the years.

Andrew Cartwright, for your editorial creativity and excellence.

Lesley Cartwright, for your creative design and layout of this book and many other projects over the years we have worked together.

Finally, I would like to thank all the **people across the world** whom God has used to build my character. As the African proverb says, "It takes a whole village to raise a child."

FOREWORD

I have known Charlie Masala for many years, having met him as he related and served the late Dr. Myles Munroe whose teachings and manner of life have inspired untold multitudes. Only eternity will fully reveal the impact his ministry has had on our generation and will continue to have on future generations.

I watched the close relationship that they shared as Father and Son and this was very inspirational to me. The last two verses in the Old Testament in Malachi 4:5-6 read as follows:

> *"Behold, I will send you Elijah the prophet before the coming of the great and dreadful day of the LORD: And he shall turn the heart of the fathers to the children, and the heart of the children to their fathers, lest I come and smite the earth with a curse"*
>
> –Malachi 4:5-6 KJV

There were 400 years of silence between the end of the Old Testament and the beginning of the New Testament where no prophetic voice was heard. John, in reflecting on Jesus Christ's life as the Son of God and Son of Man, records the following:

> *"And the Word was made flesh, and dwelt among us, (and we beheld his glory, the glory as of the only begotten of the Father,) full of grace and truth"*
>
> –John 1:14 KJV

I believe that the glory of God reaches its climax in the life of Sonship.

> *"But as many as received him, to them gave he power to become the sons of God, even to them that believe on his name"*
>
> –John 1:12 KJV

The Glory of God was revealed in Jesus Christ in Sonship. Jesus Christ is the prototype and pattern Son. The Apostle Paul said:

> *"After all, though you should have ten thousand teachers (guides to direct you) in Christ, yet you do not have many fathers. For I became your father in Christ Jesus through the glad tidings (the Gospel)"*
>
> –1 Corinthians 4:15 AMP

I saw this beautiful, heavenly Father-Son relationship being portrayed by Charlie as he served his God-given Spiritual Father, Dr. Myles Munroe. I believe every Man of God or Ascension Gift Ministry is called to be a Son to a Father and a Father to Sons.

I highly recommend this book to everyone to read and study the timeless principles of God's Word. Indeed Charlie has lived his life to leave a legacy being passed to generations. It can be said that Ambassador Charlie Masala served his generation for God's purposes as a son honouring God-given Fathers.

My prayer is that this book will be a sharp threshing instrument in God's hand to heal multitudes who were not privileged to be excellently fathered—both naturally and spiritually. Our generation needs to be healed from the deep hurts caused by dysfunctional fatherhood.

I salute you, Charlie Masala, for this timeless and inspirational work of God portrayed by your life now put in print.

In His Service,

Dr. Basil Tryon
Senior Pastor, New Covenant Fellowship
Basil Tryon Ministries
Durban, South Africa

A WORD FROM
MYLES MUNROE JR.

I have known Charlie for many years. My father, Dr. Myles Munroe, was a mentor to him and he has been like a member of the family for quite some time. Charlie is a special and gifted individual. He is a go-getter. If you need someone on your team that just knows how to make the impossible happen, that person would be Charlie. He has a calming spirit and is such a people person; I think that is his greatest trait. He knows how to motivate and empower people. Not by force or manipulation, but by being a servant leader and a man of compassion and empathy. His leadership has withstood many tests and I am happy to see that he has now chosen to pass his knowledge and experiences along by way of writing a book. His wisdom will be a positive impact on anyone that can take hold of it and I am looking forward to being one of those who are impacted as well.

A life's purpose of positively creating agents of change allowed my dad to impact and influence so many individuals and Charlie is counted in that fold. From a God-ordained meet when Charlie was a young man to becoming one of Dr. Munroe's right-hand men and an integral part of his global ministry, Charlie is more than qualified to speak on the life of such a legend. My father saw things in Charlie that Charlie could not see in himself at the time and with dad's guidance and mentorship, he helped Charlie to become the man he is today – a leader of his family, community, and his newly formed ministry. All of which have everything to do with dad's impact on his life, and I am glad he has decided to share those principles with the world.

President, Munroe Global

Vice President, The Myles and Ruth Munroe Foundation

A WORD FROM CHARISA MUNROE-WILBORN

As the saying goes, "the blood of the covenant is thicker than the water of the womb." For years I witnessed the very denotation and implication of this phrase displayed in the relationship between Charlie Masala and my parents – Drs. Myles and Ruth Munroe (affectionally called Papa Myles and Mama Ruth). Yes, it is true that sometimes the family you choose is stronger than the one you're born to. And as much as Charlie and his wife Xoli chose my parents as their family (spiritual parents), they chose him to be a part of theirs—with no reservations. So much so that Charlie's name is very similar to the biological children's—Charisa (yours truly) and Chairo.

From a young age, Charlie was as much a God-send to my dad as he was to him. Year after year after year their relationship as leader-servant-leader; father-son, and friend-friend blossomed and grew and there was nothing that could and would come between them—not even death. Even though my parents are no longer physically here, the blood covenant continues to live on in the sustained relationship between Charlie and myself. Almost instantly, we earned the affectionate names "Bro" and "Sis" as we have called each other since day one. Though they tried, no one has managed to sever the family bond that was created by those who went before. The same love, generosity, support, care, and servant-leadership that Charlie showed toward my parents, he continues to extend to me and my brother—without reservation or question.

Papa Myles and Mama Ruth needed and wanted for nothing if and when Charlie was around. They were allowed to just be the gifts that they were to the world, without any worry or unnecessary care. It was evident that my father could effectively fulfill his purpose while allowing Charlie to maximize his potential and fulfill his purpose as well—both as leaders serving leaders creating more leaders.

President, The Myles and Ruth Munroe Foundation
Vice President, Munroe Global

INTRODUCTION

The last two-and-a-half decades have been a mixture of blessings, challenges, exposure, growth, and expansion in my life—a life that went from the village of Manamani in Venda, Limpopo province, South Africa, to the uttermost parts of the world. It all began in 1990 when I watched a VHS video tape of a young, gifted Bahamian leadership consultant, Dr. Myles E. Munroe.

Back then, I never imagined that I would one day return from the Bahamas to South Africa after attending the funerals of Dr. Myles and his beloved wife, Mama Ruth Munroe. Overwhelmed with grief, anger, and disappointment at their tragic, untimely deaths, I began to reflect on our special relationship which had lasted over twenty years. As I traveled the world and interacted with people from all backgrounds who knew my relationship with Dr. Myles, all had similar questions: How did you meet Myles Munroe? What attracted him to you? What was it like to work with him? How did he spend his time offstage? What did you learn from him?

This book seeks to answer all these questions and many more. Over the years, pastors have asked me to teach at their ministries as they are fascinated with how I could serve Dr. Myles for so many years until he went home to be with the Lord.

In the words of Myles Munroe, "When God created Charlie Masala, He had me in mind!" Those words remain true today given the working relationship and journey that both Dr. Munroe and I had enjoyed until death did us part. Besides his immediate family, he had no closer relationship with anyone else in the world like the one he had with me. On numerous occasions, he referred to me as his "special son" and one who had "paid the highest price" to serve him in his vision and ministry. We became close, as father and son. I abandoned myself and my management consulting business to serve Dr. Myles Munroe for many years.

Myles Munroe wrote many books but there is a need for others to express their view of him. He never spoke about himself, and this book closes that gap. With input from esteemed contributors, it offers fascinating insights into his interactions with others, how he thought, what he did for relaxation, etc. My intimate knowledge of him compelled me to pen my thoughts on him and Mama Ruth as I had worked closely with them for the longest time.

In this book, you will learn the attitudes to embrace as you serve a senior man or woman in the church or any other environment where loyalty, honor, and respect are appreciated. You will learn about the price to be paid to serve a servant of God.

Senior leaders will learn the attitudes they should embrace as mentors. You will also discover how to prepare for your leadership succession and successor/s.

Dr. Myles Munroe was called "Mr. Purpose" for a reason. It is now clearer than ever that even his death had a purpose. Many people in the world today have gotten to hear the message of the Kingdom since his passing. My sincerest desire is that this book will inspire you to fulfill the purpose God intended for your life.

PART 1

THE EARLY YEARS

I was born in the village of Manamani in Venda, South Africa, on August 15, 1971, to a Lemba household. Venda was an "independent" homeland in northern South Africa when the country was still in the grips of apartheid. It became part of Limpopo province after apartheid ended in 1994.

The village was remote and so we were not exposed to much of what was going on in the world, especially when it came to interaction with other race groups. The whole family, including myself and seven siblings, lived in huts with a thatched roof and no windows. My mother used to make a fire for cooking in the middle of the hut and she even kept goats and chickens on one side! This is the same hut my brothers and I would use as our bedroom.

Growing up in the village, my siblings and I had the heritage of great parenting. They taught us values in life, and we looked out for and took care of each other. We respected the village elders and anyone who was ten years older than you was your "uncle or aunt." All adults played a parental role, and they had the right to reprimand, correct, and even discipline you if they caught you doing wrong. They say in Africa, "It takes a whole village to raise a child." My parents were hard workers and they instilled that culture in all seven of us. Most of my childhood was spent between school and looking after our family's livestock. My father was a boarding master and tobacco farmer, and I helped him by working in the tobacco plantation and doing some of his "piece jobs" (temporary work).

I grew up in Venda during the apartheid era and accepted Jesus Christ as my Lord and Savior when I was fifteen in 1985 at the Apostolic Faith Mission crusade planted by my late uncle, Dr. M.P. Ragimana, and Pastor M.M. Maanzwana. At the age of seventeen, I rededicated my life to God at a meeting held by an evangelist, Dr. T.S. Muligwe. I had just returned from a weekend in jail. As a political activist, I would toyi-toyi (protest) in the streets with others. I was among a group of rioters that police arrested after we looted a store.

I became involved in the ministry after being saved at that tender age. I had always loved serving and would avail myself to assist Evangelist Muligwe. He let me drive his cars, which included a BMW 6-Series, although I did not yet have a driver's license. He trusted my driving. Despite being the youngest, I was the most experienced driver on the team. I was already delivering sand, bricks, and wood with a tipper truck. I was very much involved in the ministry. I sang in the mass choir, packed the chairs, and pitched the tents because we used tents for the church services at the time.

I would crank the generators to make sure people attending a crusade had light. I was always on standby with a small tank of petrol to top up the generator when it ran dry. The lights would sometimes go off in the middle of the crusade session, so I would fill the generator's tank and the lights would come on again. In this way, we could ensure that we kept downtime and disruptions to a minimum.

Dr. Muligwe and I were close. I washed his cars, polished his shoes, and got involved wherever needed. We used to travel together, whether it was to fetch T-shirts in Tzaneen or go to Polokwane to sort out an issue with the musical instruments. We did a lot of crusades together. A crusade would last nine to ten days, and after the service, some of us would sleep in the tent. We had benches for people to sit on, but when they left, we would put all the benches together and make beds out of them.

Some of the people I worked with in that crew became pastors. I think I am the only one who didn't become a pastor at the time, along with a man called Esau Ngwana who became an advocate. Humphrey Netshifhefhe is pastoring one of the largest churches in Pretoria. Sam Tshabuse became a bishop, and he has a large church in Limpopo with a branch in Pretoria and another two branches in Johannesburg.

Thabelo Malovhele is running a church called CWC in Pretoria East. I shared a tent with these brothers. We went everywhere together to hold crusades in places like Malamulele, Tshilamba, Thengwe, Tshamulungwi, Tzaneen, Phalaborwa, and across

> My parents were hard workers and they instilled that culture in all seven of us. Most of my childhood was spent between school and looking after our family's livestock.

the border in Botswana. I also spent twelve years of my life administrating Tower of Grace, Pastor Solly Lalamani's church in Pretoria. We hosted many international events at that church, which was unheard of in Pretoria at the time. It was the first Black church in the Pretoria city center after our liberation from apartheid. These early experiences in ministry further developed my passion for serving. It nurtured a desire to encourage those involved in the Ministry of Helps and train people who work in different departments in the church. As a result, I conducted many workshops at various churches over the years.

Living Under Apartheid

Growing up under the Apartheid State in South Africa denied us better education, racial integration, and business opportunities. Blacks were not allowed in whites-only areas like public toilets, restaurants, and clubs. The only white people I saw were doctors at the district hospital, and the only Indians were shopkeepers from the closest town, Makhado (formerly Louis Trichardt). It was only when I left my local village and high school and moved to the city of Pretoria in 1991 that I realized that life was not only about my beloved rural homeland of Venda.

Arriving in Pretoria, I enrolled for a qualification in Human Resources Management at Northern Transvaal Technikon (TNT), which was part of Tshwane University of Technology. I soon began to realize and feel the real effects of apartheid as its capital city of Pretoria was a diverse city and home to most of the race groups of South Africa. I hated apartheid and could "smell racism" from a distance. Apartheid was a political and social system in South Africa during the era of White minority rule.

It enforced racial discrimination against all who were not white, mainly based on skin color and facial features. Apartheid has negatively impacted the lives of all South African children and adults. However, it has been particularly devastating psychologically, with poor self-concept, self-worth, and self-esteem still prevalent among blacks who make up most of the population in South Africa. Poverty, racism, and violence have resulted in a generation of maladjusted blacks.

Apartheid was abolished in 1994 when we gained majority rule, yet its effects linger in the minds of oppressed and oppressor alike unless something is done to counteract it. In 1995, six months before completing my studies, my life changed when I met a white lady named Isabel Agnes Schonken, in the parking lot of our university. She had come to the campus from The Council for Scientific and Industrial Research (CSIR) to visit the Technikon management. I greeted her and offered to carry her bags as she walked to the administration buildings. I accompanied her to the reception area and promised to come back later and walk her back to her car as the TNT Soshanguve campus was rough and I wanted to provide some security for her.

What I didn't know was that she was on campus to recruit two of the best Human Resources students. I only found this out when she told me so on our way back to her car. She asked me what I was studying, and I said that I was doing my final year in Human Resources Management. She immediately asked me to fax her my Curriculum Vitae (CV) and that is how I ended up working at the CSIR even though I was not the best student academically. I later asked her why she had chosen me over high academic achievers. She replied, "Your attitude!" That was the day I realized I was to excel in this way for the rest of my life. Isabel mentored me for the rest of my time at the CSIR. She became my first "white mother" and made me realize that there were white people who were not racist. I was sad to hear a few years after I left the CSIR that Isabel Schonken had been murdered during a robbery on her smallholding in Welbekend/Bronkhorstspruit, East of Pretoria, on September 28, 2009. It was tragic that she had lived to promote black people yet was murdered by a black man. A beautiful, empowering life was cut short. This deeply saddened me as my life is about promoting racial unity and teaching people to embrace diversity.

> There is so much to learn from people who are different from us. These experiences made me a richer person in my relating to others from different backgrounds.

Climbing the Corporate Ladder

After two years at the CSIR, I applied for a position at the Auditor-General of South Africa, and they invited and interviewed me for a more senior position. Arriving there in 1997, a white lady, Gail Vermeulen, welcomed me. She had been impressed with my delivery at the interview and she and her team decided to create a position especially for me.

Gail would become my second "white mother" and has remained so ever since. She mentored and trained me in Human Resources Management and Training. Gail and I would travel the provinces of South Africa, conducting Management of Diversity training at the Auditor General's provincial offices. Between us, we trained over 5000 people and consequently gained tremendous experience in leadership and management. However, the journey was not always easy. Some racist colleagues would call me names and Gail had to intervene in one of those cases.

Several years later, Gail moved to African Bank where she recruited me the first month she was there. History repeated itself when we ended up working together at an employee relations consulting firm, Integrated Labour Solutions. In 2004, I started my own Human Resources consulting company, Zoë Business Consulting, but Gail and I have remained the best of friends. Our working relationship grew to where I would visit Gail and her husband's home and would on occasion look after their house while they were away on a family holiday.

Gail has been part of every milestone in my life. Having known each other for over 23 years, we have co-authored a book, Black Son White Mother, to share our experiences and educate the corporate world on the power of diversity. While at African Bank, my boss was Mr. Frans Saunders, General Manager of the Southern Gauteng Region. He became a great friend and mentor and supported some of my trips to the leadership Summits in Nassau, Bahamas.

There is so much to learn from people who are different from us. These experiences made me a richer person in my relating to others from different backgrounds. But it was only when I was exposed to the teachings and mentorship of Bahamian Minister/Leadership Consultant and Speaker, Dr. Myles Munroe, that my life would be transformed. He introduced me to a life of possibilities I had never imagined, and we eventually traveled together to many countries on six of the seven continents of the world. My diversity exposure expanded greatly, which made me a far better person. I also learned the art of public speaking as I served him, which was never my intention in following him but a welcomed benefit, nonetheless.

Finding My Mentor

I first became aware of Dr. Myles Munroe in 1990 when I watched a video of him speaking at a conference held at the Mabee Center at Oral Roberts University (ORU) in Tulsa, Oklahoma, USA. Bishop Carlton Pearson, who ran conferences called "Azusa," organized the event. Pearson reportedly asked Dr. Munroe to speak at the conference after the invited speaker, Bishop Benson Idahosa couldn't make it.

Munroe spoke about Purpose and Vision (coming into view). To illustrate his point, he mentioned how property developers normally place billboards on vacant lots before the commencement of construction projects. Although the land is still rough and undeveloped, the billboard shows finished buildings, complete with images of parked cars and people walking about. This gives prospective buyers a glimpse of what the finished project will look like. They can then imagine themselves living or working there. Munroe further taught about the fact that God created man for a purpose and with a purpose. Watching that video as a young man from a rural village of Manamani in South Africa, I felt that this was the kind of man I would like to meet someday.

What impressed me most about Dr. Myles Munroe was not only how knowledgeable he was but also the authority with which he spoke. Here was a person of the same skin color yet was operating at a level I'd never encountered in a black person before. I only learned afterward that this was the first international exposure for him as it was his first appearance on Trinity Broadcasting Network (TBN). I just knew, no matter what, I would meet Myles Munroe one day. I nurtured a dream of having him as a mentor. Meanwhile, I watched his messages over and over, although we didn't have much of his material at the time.

I got my opportunity in 1993 when Dr. Myles Munroe came to South Africa to speak at Hatfield Christian Church (HCC) in Pretoria. It was a prominent multiracial church, a rarity in the country at the time. I was not going to miss that conference for the world. I arrived early and got a seat just two rows from the front. There were so many black people there that day that many white congregants arrived to find the prime seats already taken!

> What impressed me most about Dr. Myles Munroe was not only how knowledgeable he was but also the authority with which he spoke. I just knew I would meet him one day.

Much to my surprise, Dr. Munroe called me up on stage, along with a white guy he chose at random from the audience. Munroe used us to illustrate his message entitled "The Making of a Man," which was about how God made man from the dust of the earth. "Why do you think this dirt is better than the other dirt?" he asked the white man. "When you die both of you become dust! Just accept that we are all the same," said Munroe. He boldly spoke about the issues of race, which no one dared mention in South Africa at that time as we were still under Apartheid rule. Dr. Myles Munroe had come to Pretoria, the capital city (and capital of apartheid), as a black man when no other black man had ever set foot there invited as a speaker, let alone as the main speaker at a conference in a predominantly white church!

I sat there mesmerized by his teaching. He was the only person who appealed to my "blackness" as it related to my relationship with God. This is because most of the sermons I heard would just be raw messages about "repent or perish" or whatever; there were no sermons that reminded you that God created you in his image and that you carried his very DNA. God has placed Himself in mankind so that He can have a representation of heaven on earth.

Until I heard Dr. Myles Munroe speak, I had never heard anyone speak like that. All I knew was that you had to be born again and must forsake your sins, carry your cross, and follow Jesus. That is the only gospel I knew—at least until I found a man who explained that I came from heaven, my skin was just an "earth suit" and the real me was inside. Although I was still a student and couldn't afford much, I made sure that I bought every one of Dr. Munroe's teachings and would soak myself in them!

Myles Munroe Profile

To appreciate his capabilities and accomplishments more fully, let us look at Dr. Munroe's impressive resumé. Myles Egbert Munroe was born on April 20, 1954, in Bain Town, a low-income area in New Providence, Nassau, Bahamas, to a family of eleven children. He went on to overcome unbelievable odds to emerge as a global leader of leaders.

He was a multi-gifted minister, author, speaker, and leadership consultant who served as a mentor to millions around the world. Traveling extensively to over ninety nations, his global reach influenced all levels of society. His inspirational messages of hope, unlimited potential, and the discovery of Personal Purpose continue to transform countless lives.

Dr. Munroe authored over forty powerful, life-changing, best-selling books, which were distributed around the world in many languages. Millions have testified of the impact of his writing and the practical nature of his works.

The Gospel Today Magazine survey chose Myles Munroe as one of the Top 20 Voices of Influence in 2008-2009. Dr. Munroe's Television and Radio programs reached over 1 billion people around the world and have been seen on every continent from which he received thousands of responses weekly.

Organizational Development

Myles Munroe founded the International Third World Leaders Association (ITWLA), a global network of leaders around the world. He was also the founder and president of the International Leadership Training Institute (ILTI), and Myles Munroe International (MMI). Additionally, Dr. Munroe founded the Nassau-based ministry, Bahamas Faith Ministries International (BFMI), and Diplomat Development and Investment Company (DDIC).

Dr. Munroe built his corporations on the same philosophy he expounded to his audiences – that every human was created for a specific purpose and possesses the potential to fulfill that purpose. His distinguished client list included Fortune 500 companies, governments of the United States, Bahamas, Trinidad, Jamaica, Philippines, South Africa, Turks and Caicos, Zambia, Nigeria, Israel, Uganda, Kingdom of Swaziland, and Bermuda, along with churches, universities, schools, non-profit and athletics organizations.

For over thirty years he trained thousands of leaders in business, industry, education, government, and religion. He addressed over half a million men and women each year on personal and professional development.

Awards

Dr. Munroe was the Bahamas' youngest recipient of the Order of the British Empire (OBE) bestowed by the Queen of England, Her Majesty Queen Elizabeth II. Munroe was also the youngest recipient of the Silver Jubilee Award, the highest award bestowed by the Government of the Bahamas, both for his contribution to the civic and social development of his nation and the Caribbean region. The Trumpet Awards Foundation recognized Munroe for his contribution to global spiritual development.

Influence

As a renowned professional speaker, author, and television personality, Dr. Myles Munroe addressed critical and relevant issues affecting the full range of human social, cultural, economic, spiritual, and personal development. His passion and vision were to "Transform Followers into Leaders and Leaders into Agents of Change" and the "Maximization of Individual Potential." Dr. Munroe's message transcended barriers of age, culture, religion, occupation, race, and creed. He shared the platform with such distinguished individuals as presidents, prime ministers, monarchs, governors, corporate leaders, religious leaders, members of Congress, senators, law enforcement agencies, judicial leaders, Hollywood stars, and professional athletes. He addressed live audiences from 30 to over 300,000 and television audiences of over 1,4 billion.

Many international networks interviewed Dr. Munroe and he appeared on various shows on BET, The Tavis Smiley Show, Christian Broadcasting Network (CBN/Pat Robertson), Christian Television Network (CTN/Glenn Plummer), and Trinity Broadcasting Network (TBN/Paul Crouch).

Dr. Munroe founded and produced numerous radio and television programs that aired worldwide. His program, "Effective Living" was carried by many cable networks, including Trinity Broadcasting Network (TBN), The Inspirational Network (TIN), Cornerstone Television Network (CTN), The God Channel, Christian Broadcasting Network (CBN), Christian Television Network (CTN), Revelation Television (RTV), South African Broadcasting Corporation (SABC), Zephyr Nassau Sunshine (ZNS-BCB), Trinidad Television Network (TNT) and Crossroad's 100 Huntley in Canada.

Publishing

As a celebrated expert on personal growth, leadership, faith and spiritual development, family and relationships, and success principles, Dr. Munroe authored over seventy books. Fifteen of his titles made it to the best-seller list. His books, audio, and video tapes were translated into twelve languages, including Spanish, French, Korean, Finnish, Russian,

Ukrainian, Portuguese, and Chinese. His works include In Pursuit of Purpose, Understanding Your Potential, Releasing your Potential, Maximizing Your Potential, Becoming a Leader, The Spirit of Leadership, The Power of Vision, Rediscovering the Kingdom, The Power of Woman, The Power and Purpose of Men, The Purpose for Love and Marriage, The Glory of Living, The Burden of Freedom and most recent releases, God's Big Idea, In Charge, Benefits of Change, and Becoming a Leader, among others.

Myles Munroe was a contributing writer for various Bible editions, magazines, journals, periodicals, and newsletters, including The Believers Topical Bible, The African Cultural Heritage Bible, Charisma Life Christian Magazine, Ministries Today, Leadership and Lifestyle (London), Leadership Update, Igreja (Brazil), Purpose Magazine, and many others.

> Dr. Munroe and his wife, Ruth, who was also a public speaker (addressing women's issues), traveled as a team and taught seminars together.

Education and Community Service

Dr. Munroe earned BA and MA degrees from Oral Roberts University and the University of Tulsa and numerous honorary doctoral degrees from leading universities such as ORU and Canada Christian College. He served as an adjunct professor at the Graduate school of Theology at ORU. Dr. Munroe further served as an officer and board member of several corporations including, Colina Imperial Financial and Insurance Corp., Chairman of the Princess Margaret Hospital Foundation, Board of Regents of Oral Robert University, International Charismatic Bible Ministries, Bahamas Government Religious Tourism Board, and the University of Ft. Lauderdale.

Family Man

Dr. Munroe and his wife Ruth, who was also a public speaker (addressing women's issues), traveled as a team and taught seminars together. Both were leaders who served with sensitive hearts and an international vision. Myles and Ruth were married for over thirty years and were the proud parents of two college graduates, Charisa Munroe (BS, MSS) and Myles "Chairo" Munroe Jr. (BS, MBA).

A Timely Message Near the End of the Apartheid Regime

In the early 1990s, the days of apartheid in South Africa were numbered, and Dr. Myles Munroe visited Cape Town around the time Nelson Mandela was released from prison. Dr. Myles recognized the need to bring a message of unity and reconciliation to the hurting people of the nation. Some years later, he told of how he was very much aware of the hostile situation in the country and knew what he was getting into. The apartheid regime had told whites that they were superior to black people and so had to live apart from them.

Dr. Myles's assignment and burden were to set oppressed black people free by helping them realize that God had created them in His image, that they were valuable, and were not to be the subjects of oppression.

Dr. Munroe related how the situation here made him weep when he realized that so many Black South Africans were poor and being treated like slaves and not benefiting from the farms they were working on. On a visit to Cape Town, he stayed at a hotel where the black staff members were surprised to see a white pastor, the late Dr. Neville McDonald of Good Hope Christian Centre, having conversations with and serving a black man from the Bahamas. No black man could stay at that hotel, let alone have a conversation there with a white man! The workers wanted to know who this black man was and how he came to be treated in this special way.

The Roebert Family

The senior pastor of Hatfield Christian Church, Ed Roebert, was one of the pioneers of racial harmony in South Africa. He welcomed people of all races and was open to having a black minister stand in his pulpit. This surprised me because people expected white pastors to be "verkrampte," an Afrikaans term meaning rigid and conservative. However, Pastor Ed recognized that Dr. Myles Munroe was very gifted, talented, and wise. Pastor Ed invited Myles Munroe to speak annually at Hatfield Christian Church. Pastor Ed's openness to the message of inclusion of black people enabled me to become close with Pastor Ed.

Africa owes a debt of gratitude to the Roebert family for introducing Myles Munroe to this continent. The history of Dr. Myles Munroe is not complete without a mention of the Roebert brothers—Bernard Victor Roebert (1936-2020), a pioneer of Christian television in South Africa, and Edmund "Ed" Roebert (1939-1997), the senior pastor of Hatfield Christian Church. Pastor Neville McDonald (1953-2020), who first hosted Myles Munroe in Cape Town, was a son-in-law of Dr. Fred Roberts

(1932-2017), who founded Durban Christian Centre. Myles Munroe International/Munroe Global continued to enjoy the relationship with the Roebert family as Dr. Myles spoke at Choose Life Church, founded and led by Ps. Ed Roebert's son, John Roebert until Dr. Myles passed away in 2014. The relationship has also seen Myles Jr. and Charisa Munroe appear at Choose Life Church as guest speakers on several occasions. Bernard Roebert's son, Dr. André Roebert, who is the president of the Faith Broadcasting Network, East London, South Africa, also hosted Dr. Myles Munroe several times.

Healing a Wounded Nation

In 1994, I was one of the leaders of the Student Christian Fellowship (SCF) at Technikon Northern Transvaal (TNT). We had been cultivating a relationship with Hatfield Christian Church, which had been hosting Dr. Munroe. However, I was concerned that Dr. Munroe was focusing on a predominantly white church. I felt that black people, especially students, also needed to hear his message so they too could be delivered. I decided to organize a conference on campus with Dr. Myles Munroe as the keynote speaker.

Dr. Myles believed that both blacks and whites were living under a yoke of oppression. The white man thought he was oppressing the black man, yet whites were also victims due to the response of those they oppressed. Munroe said both groups were sick, both were oppressed. I reasoned that if young black people could get that message, it would spread rapidly, and everyone would start to feel a sense of self-worth. South Africa held its first non-racial election in April 1994, but people were more vocal about topical issues with politicians than with the Church. The narratives centered on issues of equality, equal access to the economy, equal rights, humane treatment of others, and the right to vote. This is where Dr. Myles Munroe played a significant role as he was very bold to deal head-on with sensitive issues in South Africa.

Hatfield Christian Church invited Dr. Munroe to speak each year from 1993 onwards. Sadly, Pastor Ed Roebert died suddenly of a heart attack in July 1997 at a Christian rally in Pretoria. I was with Dr. Munroe at his office in the Bahamas when we received the news about the death of Pastor Ed. October 1997 was also the last time Dr. Munroe spoke at the Faith Promise Conference, which was held annually at Hatfield Christian Church.

The new leadership did not like his message titled "Vision Beyond the Visionary." He taught that they should honor the legacy and spirit of the founding father of the church, Pastor Ed Roebert. This meant showing honor to his wife, Auntie Pal Roebert, and the Roebert sons. For some reason, they never embraced the idea, which led Dr. Munroe to say that if they ever saw him there again it meant he had not heard from God!

Dr. Myles felt he was not going to betray the founding father and his succession wishes. Ps. Ed had chosen his son, John Roebert, as his successor. Ps. John instead became the founder and current senior pastor of Choose Life Church. True to his word, Dr. Myles never set foot again in Hatfield Christian Church until he was recalled to his home country of heaven on November 9, 2014.

Munroe Addresses Students

Before the conference was held at HCC in 1994, I approached Pastor Ed Roebert to ask if he could arrange for Dr. Munroe to address students at Technikon Northern Transvaal. If he could do a morning session and another in the afternoon on a Saturday, he could still speak at Hatfield Christian Church in the evening. I promised that if Pastor Ed could give us Myles Munroe on Campus, we would fill the Gencor Hall with attendees. To my delight, Pastor Ed was excited about the idea.

I will always remember the day Myles Munroe visited the Technikon Northern Transvaal—Soshanguve Campus on October 14, 1995. The hall was packed—six thousand people! He did two sessions that day, the first session being his message titled, "Nobody Knows You Like the Manufacturer." That message empowered us all.

He pointed out that a manufacturer knows its products better than anyone else. Therefore, we should not believe the opinions of anyone who is not our Manufacturer. The only opinion that matters comes from the One who created you, gave you purpose, and liberated you.

Dr. Munroe spoke on "The Five Principles for Personal Success" in his second session. The first principle is Purpose, based on Genesis 1:26 which says, Then God said, "Let us make mankind in our image, in our likeness, so that they may rule over the fish in the sea and the birds in the sky, over the livestock and all the wild animals, and over all the creatures that move along the ground" (NIV). He explained that God created everything, including mankind, with a purpose. He said that if a mosquito has a purpose, then surely you have an even greater purpose. Success principle number two is Potential. Whatever God wants from you He has already put in you. It is not from the outside in; it is already in you. Don't look far from yourself because God has put that greatness within you. That is potential. Then he spoke about principle number three—Planning. God has given you the potential to fulfill your purpose, but you must plan to realize that purpose. He quoted from the Bible, saying that a man has many plans in his heart, but God's purpose will prevail (Proverbs 19:21). He said that as you pursue your plans, make sure that you plan according to God's purpose for your life so that your plans and purpose are aligned.

Success principle number four is Perseverance. Munroe said you must be willing to persevere because life is not always easy. A school-teacher in his homeland of the Bahamas once called him a "monkey" and said he would "not amount to anything."

Dr. Myles turned this incident into a powerful principle. He emphasized that not everyone will recognize our value or God-given purpose in life. That is why you must persevere even if you go through "hell and high water." Using the students as an example, he said that if you fail a subject, you must simply repeat it until you pass.

Those kinds of things happen but if you persevere you will ultimately emerge as a victor. Dr. Munroe discussed Prayer as his fifth principle for personal success and he concluded the afternoon session with prayer. I have taught these five principles—Purpose, Potential, Planning, Perseverance, and Prayer—over one hundred times, although I have since added another three principles. Using the story of my life, I also speak about Positive Attitude, Principles, and Power. You must have principles in life. If you don't stand for something you will fall for anything. And when you have power, you must remember that you were given that power to administer grace. You were not given that power to dominate other people but to bring healing. You can bring hope to people—even as an employee. That is the ultimate responsibility that comes with power.

A Personal Invitation

I had been very hands-on as Master of Ceremonies and the Technikon event was a success. At the end of the second session, I approached Dr. Munroe and asked him if he would mentor me. I did not fully understand what mentorship would entail but knew I wanted to officially be close to him so I could learn as much as possible. He said, "Sure," and handed me a business card with his home phone number on it, saying I could call or write him there. My dream was finally coming to pass.

Something strange happened to me the very Monday after Myles Munroe had spoken at our campus. I wrote a test on Management of Training (one of my weaker subjects in the Human Resources Diploma course) and scored 84%! That was the first time I got such a high mark. Unfortunately, I did not make a copy of that test because I mailed the original together with a letter that I wrote to Dr. Munroe. I explained that my high score was a result of his motivation.

Potential: whatever God wants from you He has already put in you. It's not from the outside in; it is already in you. Don't look far from yourself because God has put greatness within you.

I began to write him more often and he would write back. Due to the distance involved, we would sometimes meet in person before each other's letters arrived. I made it my assignment to find out his travel plans so I could be at the airport to greet him every time he landed in South Africa. All those years that Dr. Myles Munroe landed here I would be there to meet him each time. Whoever hosted Dr. Munroe never had a problem with me being there. They knew Dr. Myles liked me and he would say, "That's my son. That's my boy!" He would single me out from the crowd whenever I was able to attend an event where he was teaching. He often traveled with his wife, mom Ruth Munroe, and would always carry their bags or assist them in any way possible when they arrived at the airport. The relationship just grew from there.

In July 1997, I took my very first trip outside of Africa to attend a conference in the Bahamas. This was before Dr. Munroe delivered his "Vision beyond the Visionary" message at Hatfield Christian Church later that year. It was a "faith trip" and Pastor Ed Roebert sponsored me with a thousand rand for spending money and accommodation. I was going to the Bahamas! I was going to see my mentor! Finally, I would get to see Bain Town and Nassau and all the places he had spoken of. I was even prepared to "sleep under the stars," as long as I was where Myles Munroe was.

Arriving there, we stayed at a very low-class, low-budget hotel. I then stayed with some guys who came with Stuart Agnew, a youth pastor from Hatfield. He was one of the speakers at the Youth Alive Conference in 1997. I remember paying about thirty dollars for three nights' accommodation. Dr. Munroe approached the Bahamas Faith Ministries

International (BFMI) youth pastor, Dave Burrows (who succeeded Dr. Myles Munroe as Senior Pastor) to arrange accommodation for me. Ps. Dave's PA, Rosie Smith, was able to accommodate me at her home. She is a white German lady who married a black pilot in the Bahamas. They fed me and I stayed at their house for the rest of the trip. It was a blessing because I no longer had to worry about transportation and other expenses, as Rosie and I would travel to and from the conference together.

My first trip to the Bahamas was very eventful and a turning point in my life. When I arrived, Dr. Munroe gave me that "signature hug" and said, "My son from South Africa! I am so glad you finally made it to your home, the Place where God lives." He shared a lot of his heart on that trip. He called me to his office, gave of his precious time, and handed me some books as a gift. We began forging a deep bond.

As a village boy, I had not been exposed to restaurants, so I ate whatever Dr. Munroe ate. When we went out to eat, I would just say, "I'll have what he's having!" I accepted whatever he recommended because I was dedicated to learning all I could from my mentor. However, the news of Pastor Ed Roebert's death on July 5, 1997, overshadowed the trip. I remember Dr. Myles cried that day. He loved Pastor Ed very much. Pastor Ed was not sick, so his sudden passing was an unexpected blow.

He was participating as a member of the Organizing Committee of the Global Consultation on World Evangelism (GCOWE), in the March for Jesus 97 event in the capital city when he collapsed from a cardiac arrest. I was also devastated because Pastor Ed had partly sponsored my trip to the Bahamas, which had enabled me to become more involved with Dr. Myles Munroe.

Leadership for Change

Part of my learning involved reading everything Dr. Myles Munroe had written. I noticed he always dedicated a message to Third World people and addressed the Third World mentality in his books. That is what he lived for, and I always got excited about the idea that somehow Dr. Myles was pan-African in his approach and mentality.

Dr. Munroe began speaking to me about the International Third World Leaders Association (ITWLA). He founded the organization when he was thirty years old, together with several other leaders, some of whom have also since passed on. He felt that God had called him to bring deliverance to people being excluded from the Industrial Revolution and its benefits. These are the people and countries referred to as "Third World." He defined Third World as a mentality. It is a mentality because people with Third World thinking are also found in the First World and Second World.

He urged me to join ITWLA immediately, which I did while on that trip to the Bahamas. Since its inception, ITWLA has grown to be represented in over sixty nations with Trustees on most continents. The organization's vision is to bring change to the world through leadership.

Myles Munroe was very conscious of his ancestry. He was born in poverty in The Bahamas. However, he knew he came from Africa and had a special love for her, even though Third World people are found on all continents. He knew that Africa was the "Cradle of Humankind," yet its people were still being oppressed. He felt they needed deliverance and not just economic but mental too. He believed that if you are freed mentally then all other freedoms become easy.

In his book, Burden of Freedom, Dr. Munroe discusses how most Third World countries are the product of colonization, although most have gained their independence. He reveals that being politically freed or gaining independence is not true freedom. Being freed from slavery does not mean you are free from slavery in your thinking. Even though we are no longer "colonized," our minds are still not free. This is because freedom is the ability to conceptualize something and be allowed to actualize it in a conducive environment. This is not the case in many Third World countries.

Myles Munroe was well suited to dealing with African problems and the African struggle because he understood the context. He had lived under colonization, oppression, and subjugation—conditions created to marginalize people. First World people could not understand it because they had not lived under it. Dr. Munroe understood the mind of the oppressed. Each time he came to these countries he wanted to break that barrier of mental oppression. Again, he had a hunger to liberate oppressed people. He understood that oppression was not just oppression of Blacks; he knew that he also had to help the people who believed they were superior to those they were oppressing. In the end, I can say he was just targeting humans in general.

When it comes to Africa, there is a clear line between what Dr. Myles Munroe and other leadership experts like John Maxwell address. Maxwell deals with the techniques of leadership, while Munroe deals with the psychology and spirit of leadership. These are two vastly different concepts.

Dr. Myles Munroe was so well suited to addressing African oppression because he could associate it, having grown up in the Bahamas while it was still a British colony and having lived under British oppression himself. The Bahamas only gained her majority rule/ independence on July 10, 1973.

Humble Beginnings

ITWLA's footprint in Africa started small, as Dr. Munroe had only impacted South Africa and Zimbabwe by 1997. His relationship with Zimbabwe was primarily through Archbishop Papa Ezekiel Guti, who became the first ITWLA Trustee on the continent.

> My relationship with Dr. Munroe strengthened and deepened each time we met. He was always excited to see me and I was also excited to see him.

Pastor Ed Roebert in Pretoria, South Africa, was not in the ITWLA network but was the first person in Gauteng (formerly Transvaal province) to host Dr. Myles Munroe in 1993. Ps. Neville McDonald, who founded Good Hope Christian Centre (GHCC) in Cape Town together with his wife, Ps. Wendy McDonald, was the first host to host Dr. Munroe in the Western Cape Province. This was in 1990. I only met Myles Munroe three years later but would certainly have tried to attend that conference in Cape Town had I known about it. His second visit to our region occurred in 1998 because of a relationship Myles Munroe had with the international Bible teacher, Dr. Elijah Maswanganyi. He brought Dr. Munroe to eSwatini (Swaziland) at the invitation of a Prince who was the Deputy

Prime Minister of Swaziland at the time. Dr. Myles met with the king's mother but not the king himself on that visit. When I became involved in ITWLA at the leadership level, I kept Swaziland in mind, although my broader target was the continent of Africa.

ITWLA was not so active in South Africa, even though we had almost twenty Trustees at one time. I remember when the likes of Dr. John Tibane, Pastor Nick Mosupi, and other prominent leaders joined ITWLA. Most were part of the organizing committee for Dr. Munroe's visits to South Africa. As you know, people fall away because they sometimes start enthusiastically or end up in a battle for control.

My relationship with Dr. Munroe strengthened and deepened each time we met. He was always excited to see me and I was also excited to see him. Whenever he came to South Africa with his family, my job was to carry their bags and make sure they were comfortable. I was taught to serve from a young age. While I was still in Venda at Dr. Muligwe's Divine Life Ministries/Kingdom Life Christian Centre, we would go to crusades and sleep in tents, carrying chairs, benches, and whatever else was needed. That spirit of serving stayed with me and I believe it is part of the reason Myles Munroe liked me so much. His wife, mom Ruth Munroe, and children, Myles Jr. and Charisa Munroe also became fond of me. Their family was and still is my family!

Global Leadership Mandate

Since my first visit to the Bahamas in 1997, I have returned to attend the Global Leadership Summits held each year in November. I sometimes visited three times a year, depending on commitments. The Lord would always provide for the trip, regardless of cost. At one stage, the Office of the Auditor-General of South Africa where I was working sponsored my trip. African Bank also sponsored several of my visits to the Bahamas. I funded the balance of my trips and God always supplied the means to do so.

Dr. Myles Munroe, The International Third World Leaders Association, and Bahamas Faith Ministries International launched the Global Leadership Summit initially as an international conference for Christian leaders to effect positive change in their nations. Summit Speakers spoke on the leadership skills of Jesus and time-tested biblical principles. The organizers had renamed the conference Global Leadership Forum, by the time Dr. Myles passed.

The International Third World Leaders Association and Myles Munroe International then began to jointly host the event. The idea was to gather leaders and not just Christian leaders from around the world who had a passion for leadership development, particularly in Third World countries. The conference provided a place where delegates could be rallied, inspired, and empowered. They would return to their countries with a fiery determination to get involved in leadership development, politics, business, and so on.

Although ITWLA represented Third World countries, many delegates came from First World nations, hence the decision to have dual hosting. To be honest, most people came there for Myles Munroe. They came from all walks of life, mostly by his invitation. Dr. Munroe built that organization. People would arrive from Africa, America, Asia, Australia, Sweden, Papua New Guinea, Europe—all the different countries and continents. As interest in the conference grew, Dr. Munroe felt the need to change its format.

Whenever he spoke about the Global Leadership Summit during his travels, companies wanted to send employees to attend. That is why it could no longer be an overtly Christian event even though our values remain unchanged. Everything about the Global Leadership Summit, including promotional materials, had to appear as neutral as possible. The keynote speakers would still be dynamic leaders having strong, biblical, time-tested principles. However, their message had to change from preaching style to corporate style. The Global Leadership Summit had come of age and would continue to impact pastors and leaders from all over the world for years to come.

International Association of Kingdom Churches & Ministries (IAKCM)

Leadership Development and Training was the heartbeat of Dr. Myles Munroe's calling. Over the years, he received numerous requests from pastors around the world to provide spiritual covering. However, he felt that he didn't have enough time at his disposal to effectively father and spiritually cover all the pastors who were sending requests. Consequently, he decided to form IAKCM under the auspices of the ITWLA, and have Dr. Richard Pinder and Dr. Peter Morgan lead it.

PART 2

WORKING WITH
MYLES MUNROE
Becoming A Servant Leader
From Elijah to Elisha

The idea of serving Dr. Myles Munroe had been in my spirit since 1995 and I took every opportunity to do so. In my mind, I never anticipated benefiting from the relationship but just wanted to ease his workload. I felt that Dr. Myles was a part of my purpose for living. We both felt that we were meant for each other. Working with Dr. Myles didn't feel like work; I felt like I could just be myself around him. I was willing to pay any price for that and I did without any regrets.

Self-Abandonment

I believe that for any servant of God whom God has called to grow and be able to achieve the vision God gave them, they need other men and women who are willing to abandon themselves for a greater vision. Dr. Myles Munroe called it a catalyst vision—a vision that submits to another vision to get the job done. Catalyst vision requires one visionary to submit their vision to another man for the sake of their vision.

Referring to me, Dr. Myles used the term "self-abandonment," saying that no one else had ever abandoned themselves to the vision God gave him of "Transforming Followers into Leaders and Leaders into Agents of Change" and that of bringing change through leadership.

In 2010, I abandoned my business in Management Consulting to serve Dr. Myles Munroe, thereby losing income. Bear in mind that I didn't ask for a job or was given a post. My office was based in South Africa while Dr. Munroe's was in the Bahamas. This was, of course, a costly decision as I started falling behind with my financial obligations, including my home loan. I remember dealing with my lovely bank threatening foreclosure and repossession. It never really moved me as I knew I was using stubborn faith. After two years, Dr. Myles realized I was serving him full-time without pay and so he decided that I should be compensated. I recommend you "Don't try this at home" unless you have an inspired word from the Lord.

In my case, serving Dr. Myles Munroe was an issue of conviction and response to a calling. I believe this was from God because through this act of obedience we were able to reach almost ten new nations in Africa. Of course, the timing was of critical importance because Dr. Myles would transition within the space of seven years. I learned that God could sustain his servants because after that act of obedience I started experiencing God's provision at a much higher level.

One of Dr. Myles' usual utterances to me was: "May you never lack anything in your life." I remember when he turned sixty in April 2014, and I asked him what I could get him for a birthday present. He answered, "You have already given me the greatest gift you could give, which is yourself." I was humbled. Right then I got a revelation on giving—there is no gift you will ever give which will be more special than giving of yourself. Most of us pride ourselves in giving amounts like 10%, 25%, or 50% when God is just looking for us. The key is in the Kingdom; you don't give just percentages; you give 100% of yourself. In the Kingdom, you make yourself, and not your possessions, a living sacrifice. Many of us try and please God by giving him a tithe of our income and then God is not involved with the remaining ninety percent of our income and our lives. That is religion. In the Kingdom, the earth is the Lord's and the fullness thereof. We own nothing. Everything belongs to the King, although we have access to all of God's resources.

"So Elijah went from there and found Elisha son of Shaphat. He was plowing with twelve yoke of oxen, and he himself was driving the twelfth pair. Elijah went up to him and threw his cloak around him. Elisha then left his oxen and ran after Elijah. "Let me kiss my father and mother goodbye," he said, "and then I will come with you." "Go back," Elijah replied. "What have I done to you?" So Elisha left him and went back. He took his yoke of oxen and slaughtered them. He burned the plowing equipment to cook the meat and gave it to the people, and they ate. Then he set out to follow Elijah and became his servant"

–1 Kings 19:19-21 (NIV)

One of the problems of progressive leadership is the inability or unwillingness to serve others. Elisha surrendered his agenda, submitted himself to Elijah, shouldered Elijah's burden, and supported Elijah's vision. A culture of honor and respect is critical to good succession.

With an undermining mentality, there cannot be a successive transfer of leadership from one generation to the next. May you possess the spirit of service as Elisha did, so that you can be propelled to greatness. My prayer is that as you read this passage God will show you servants/leaders and people you can submit to, honor, and serve. The Bible says that *he who refreshes others will also be refreshed* (Proverbs 11:25).

Climbing the Corporate Ladder

> I would plan Dr. Myles Munroe's next trip. It was also my job to decide which ministries, governments and government entities he could address. I would then try to ensure that it happened.

I was still a student when I first became involved in the ministry with Dr. Myles Munroe. I landed my first job at the Council for Scientific and Industrial Research (CSIR) in Pretoria, earning "peanuts" for about eight months. After that, I got a permanent position at the Office of the Auditor-General of South Africa. From there I moved to African Bank, working as a Human Resources Practitioner, a Generalist.

While working full-time, I was also doing most of the work for Myles Munroe International and ITWLA after hours. I would plan Dr. Myles Munroe's next trip—where he should go, what we should focus on, and suitable themes for his presentations, etc. It was also my job to decide which ministries, governments, and government entities he could address. I would then try to ensure that it happened.

In 2004, I opened a company called Zoe Business Consulting after Dr. Munroe encouraged me to start my own business. It focused on management development, management consulting programs, team building, and everything else related to Human Resources. African Bank still employed me at the time, and I didn't leave right away because the bank felt I could still add value. I only resigned after my employer accepted my proposal to act as a consultant rather than be on the payroll.

This turned out to be a wonderful experience. I had a good manager who supported me. He gave me a retrenchment package and a contract. My first client was my former employer, so I didn't have to go out and struggle to drum up business for my new company! I ended up having more time on my hands than before. I served out that first retainer agreement and African Bank renewed it several times after that.

After I joined ITWLA in July 1997, Dr. Munroe began to take me to Board meetings. These were not just Trustee meetings, but Board meetings with senior Board members. He recommended me as a Trustee but because I was still young, he created a Junior Trustee level. However, my responsibilities far exceeded my title due to the scope of work I had for him and the organization. We would arrange a month of speaking engagements for Dr. Munroe throughout Africa and further abroad. We also chartered a jet to transport him to different places using Johannesburg as a base each time he visited the continent.

All that work gave me much to report on. Whenever I arrived in the Bahamas at the Board and Trustee meetings, Dr. Myles would say, "Okay Charlie, give us a South African report" or "I need you to come and speak tonight." Initially, I was not sure what he was expecting and was not well prepared. But because he would do this often, I realized that when I went to the Bahamas, I had better have a report ready.

Once bitten, twice shy! I began to take the role more seriously and prepared my reports before I left home. My reporting grew from just speaking to doing proper presentations and I ended up delivering these presentations many times. Admittedly, it was intimidating, as my audience included leaders from governments, businesses, and civil societies all over the world. Sometimes a prime minister and his deputy were present. South African governmental ministers would be there when I was reporting on South Africa!

The Africa Regional Office

In 2008/9, I felt that God was nudging me to focus on serving my mentor even more. I loved Dr. Myles Munroe. It was my heart to serve him. We had office space in Brooklyn, Pretoria, which was operating under the name of the church in the Bahamas, Bahamas Faith Ministries. As Myles Munroe was traveling to South Africa twice yearly, I got the idea to establish a Myles Munroe International office in Centurion, Pretoria, which I did in 2011. I remember when Dr. Munroe saw the office for the first time. I had set up everything without telling him. He found it fully furnished and operational. He just sat in a chair and wept. Both He and Mama Ruth were very emotional that night. He spoke about how we could affect the whole of Africa from this office and how strategic it would be for his work. They left happy and fulfilled.

My next strategy was to focus on engaging new hosts. My passion had always been for Myles Munroe to be here for the people, instead of only going to the big churches. I started taking him to the people. He began speaking in smaller venues because he could reach people in those places that he wouldn't normally reach. All these came about because I believe God placed it in my heart to do so. My work was aligned with Dr. Myles Munroe's vision and purpose. Each time he landed in South Africa I would meet him at the airport and hand him a specially designed itinerary for his trip. The best recognition he ever gave me was that he would always say, "What would I do without Charlie? I believe that God had me in mind when he created you!"

That was the most beautiful expression of how close we had become. Our hearts were truly knitted together.

I remember when Dr. Munroe saw the office for the first time. I had set up everything without telling him. He found it fully furnished and operational. He just sat in a chair and wept. Both he and Mama Ruth were emotional that night.

The Centurion office was a giant leap forward for Myles Munroe International. It all started when Bahamas Faith Ministries hosted the Global Leadership Summit in 1997. Dr. Munroe appointed me as a signatory and one of the directors. In the early years, Dr. Munroe only had the name of the church, Bahamas Faith Ministries, which is why the office in South Africa was named after it. But things changed over time.

When we opened the Centurion office, we decided we could no longer operate under the Bahamas Faith Ministries name because it was based in the Bahamas. The new office was geared towards Myles Munroe's work in Africa, to which we added Asia and Middle East activities.

A conversation with Dr. Myles led to the formation of Myles Munroe International (MMI) and ITWLA locally. In my capacity as Managing Director, I started building both Myles Munroe International, which was mostly me together with Dr. Munroe, and ITWLA, which was me and the other Trustees we recommended. Since taking over the two organizations, I started making ITWLA more active.

Expanding Our Reach

From 1997 to 2010, Dr. Myles Munroe would come to South Africa for eight or ten days at a time and mostly focus on speaking engagements in Johannesburg. When I started getting more involved, I began taking him to places in other provinces including Venda, Limpopo, and KwaZulu-Natal. We also went to Namibia a few times but from 2012 I started to feel that we must expand our reach beyond Southern Africa. I had a responsibility to create working relationships in all these different countries.

We initially went as far as Ghana, Nigeria, and Kenya, with an eye on reaching northernmost countries like Egypt and Ethiopia. Through consistent efforts, we touched South Africa, Namibia, Swaziland (at king's level), Botswana, Zambia, Malawi, Tanzania, Uganda, Burundi, and Nigeria. Even before my time, Dr. Munroe was well known in Nigeria because Pastor Ghandi Olaoye was actively promoting his ministry there. We only began getting more established as an office in Africa when I became involved full-time. The commitment to establishing MMI and ITWLA in most of those countries has continued to this day. We added Asia and I started organizing engagements in Indonesia and Hong Kong.

Meanwhile, ITWLA only had Trustees in South Africa, so we continued to recruit people as members. We recommended those who were dedicated to the cause as Trustees. Consequently, many people got involved as supporters and Trustees.

A New Era

In my view, the legacy of Myles Munroe has four aspects: 1. Integrity, purity, and holiness, 2. The Kingdom message, 3. Purpose, and 4. Leadership. Dr. Munroe was a man of integrity and purity. He emphasized clean living and I am convinced that one of the most important books he wrote is The Power of Character in Leadership.

Dr. Myles defined character as the moral force of leadership. He prized character over gifting, skills, and talents.

In continuing the legacy of Myles Munroe, it was decided to change the name of Myles Munroe International to Munroe Global Incorporated. ITWLA still exists as a separate entity, and I have continued to be responsible for both in my region. An unavoidable slowdown occurred after Dr. Munroe passed but we have been working on continuing to grow the organization with his son, Myles Jr., as its chairman.

My relationship with the Munroe family stretches back to 1993. Mama Ruth had already met me in South Africa, but I only got to know the children later as they were still young. Myles "Chairo" Jr. was around nine or ten years old and Charisa eleven or so. I remember Myles Jr. playing basketball in the churchyard with the other kids during the Youth Alive Conference. They had a basketball championship of some kind on that Saturday. I just greeted him and didn't say much because he was only ten years old. He remembers that because he tells people he has known me from an early age.

Myles Jr. and Charisa finished school in the Bahamas and then went to study at university in the USA. They spent most of their teenage years there. Myles Jr. worked in the organization with his dad from around 2008/9. By the time Dr. Myles Munroe passed, he had worked with him for at least five years. When Dr. Munroe was away from home, he would often talk to Myles Jr. and Charisa via Skype. Dr. Myles and Mama Ruth wanted me to mentor Chairo and Charisa, so I suggested they start coming to South Africa. I remember Mama Munroe liked that idea very much and Dr. Myles said we should make it happen. We usually budgeted for an entourage of several people that would accompany Dr. Munroe, so I started adding Myles Jr. and Charisa to the list. The idea was to let them come here because they were not kids anymore but grownups. They had to see what was happening for themselves and figure out how they could get involved with the work.

I remember the first time Chairo arrived in South Africa in 2010. He was so jetlagged that he slept the whole day! However, he was excited about the trip and even went on a safari. That was my first real introduction to him, and we spent much time talking. He and Charisa fell in love with South Africa and Africa. They said that they felt more at home here than in the Bahamas! My wife, Xoli, and I drew close to them, especially since Dr. Myles' and Mom Ruth's passing. The names Charlie and Xoli became household names in the Munroe family. I have become closer with Charisa and realized she was more like Dr. Myles in terms of her outgoing personality and Chairo is more reserved like his mom. Our relationship grew, not just because their parents encouraged them to get to know me better, but because they got to know me firsthand. Dr. Myles and Mom Ruth always used to say that if there was somebody who understood what we were doing, who had our hearts, and who supported us one hundred and fifty percent, it was Charlie and Xoli.

Each time they came here they knew they were going to be with Charlie and Xoli. That is the relationship I had with the family, and it was an awesome one. Dr. Myles and Mama Ruth would spend hours with me after meetings in the different countries.

We would be awake in our hotel rooms sometimes up to 3 a.m. Dr. Myles would look very British in his shorts and long socks and Mama Ruth would be in her pajamas with me there. That is the kind of relationship we had. I think I'm probably the only person who has ever seen Mama Ruth without her dressing hair. We were family.

> Dr. Myles and Mama Ruth wanted me to mentor Chairo and Charisa, so I suggested they start coming to South Africa. I remember Mama Munroe liked the idea very much, and Dr Myles said we should make it happen.

By 2009, Chairo had finished studying and wanted to stay in the US. However, when he couldn't find a job, his dad suggested he come back and work with him. Chairo felt it was the right thing to do and he returned to the Bahamas. A year later, I suggested Chairo come to South Africa and include him in our budget so he could be part of that trip. I am glad we did that because if Myles Jr. had not gotten involved from 2009 to 2014 when his parents passed, he would have had little exposure to the global work that Dr. Myles Munroe did. The relationship with me and with others and other organizations would not have been strengthened as they were.

Working from his office at the church, Myles. Jr. began to learn how the organization was run and to understand how Dr. Munroe's busy schedule functioned.

Charisa was also involved as she had started traveling with her dad. She joined the mentoring program and read his books, so they were both up to speed. If it hadn't happened the way it did, the organization may have been flung into confusion when its founder passed unexpectedly.

Today, Myles Jr. and Charisa are very much involved in the organization as leaders of the different entities. The first thing they did was acknowledge that they were not Myles Munroe. They were not going to attempt to replace him. I think this was wise. Just before we buried Dr. Munroe, I said to Myles Jr. that he and Charisa should continue to visit Africa and that people would be receptive to them. I am sure he didn't give it much thought because of all they had to deal with at the time.

Nonetheless, I assured them that my wife and I would be there for them. Our relationship did not need to change just because their parents were no longer here. And that is just what we did. We embraced them both as we had Dr. Myles and Mama Ruth.

Since then, Myles "Chairo" Jr. Munroe and Charisa Munroe have kept coming back to Africa, sometimes twice a year. They were even among the guest speakers at our marriage retreats. The power couple had raised them, which gave them valuable insights into marriage. Meanwhile, Myles Jr. and Charisa had been contemplating a new direction and wanted to honor their parents' legacy. That is when the Myles and Ruth Munroe Foundation was born.

The Foundation's purpose is to become an extension of and to support Dr. Munroe's work. The Foundation focuses on education because the eradication of ignorance was closest to his heart. The Foundation would also help support ITWLA and the other organizations that Dr. Munroe left behind.

Dr. Myles & Mama Ruth's Last Month on Planet Earth

Africa was close to Dr. Myles Munroe's heart. The year 2014 was indeed special and in hindsight one is tempted to think the heavens allowed us a special final year with both Dr. Myles and Mama Ruth. It was the first time that Dr. Myles and Mama Ruth came to South Africa four times in the space of one year. The first visit was in April for a trip that covered Johannesburg and Harare, Zimbabwe. The second visit was after an invitation from former president Jacob Zuma for his Presidential Inauguration on May 24. Dr. Myles next arrived in August for his regular trips covering the Southern part of Africa, with his fourth trip taking place from October 7 to October 31, 2014. The October trips usually lasted a month, and I was privileged for the few preceding years to spend much time with them both as we moved every second or third day from city to city, country to country.

The October 2014 trip began in South Africa where we ministered in Witbank, Pretoria, Johannesburg, and Durban. The second leg covered eSwatini (Swaziland, including a visit to His Majesty King Mswati III), Manzini-Matshapa, Sun City in North West Province (Royal Bafokeng nation with a special visit to the King and the Queen Mother). The 3 rd and last leg went north of our border into Tanzania, Kenya, Bujumbura, Burundi, and Libreville, Gabon. I remember that all these trips were special as Dr. Munroe was able to speak into the lives of the kings, presidents, and captains of industry in each country.

Visiting the Swazi King

The trip to eSwatini to meet His Majesty King Mswati III was special. We were guests of the king and were invited to have dinner with His Majesty at the royal palace. According to the king, something very unusual and special occurred that night. We had just arrived and were getting out of the car when there was a huge thunderclap. It rained briefly and stopped. His Majesty said that this was a sign our visitation was blessed.

That night we sat around a large dinner table with many chefs and servers in attendance. We were flanked by the princes, with the Prime Minister and Deputy Prime Minister also present. After the introductions, we had a great time, and the food was delicious. I remember my starter was shark fin soup. It was the first time I had ever heard of such a soup let alone taste it! This was indeed a special royal menu. I found His Majesty the King to be a very approachable and friendly person who liked shaking hands and engaging guests each time we visited the palace. I had the opportunity to meet him on all three occasions we were there. For some reason, he liked me and always wanted me around when he was to meet Dr. Myles in private.

After dinner, the King asked to see Dr. Myles and he asked for Mama Ruth and me to remain in the palace. They discussed many things that night. It was clear that Dr. Myles' visit and his inputs on issues of national leadership were particularly important for His Majesty's work and solving some of the challenges the nation was facing. I remember that the meeting started around 11 p.m. and concluded around 3 a.m.

One of the important outcomes of the meeting was that Dr. Munroe coined a phrase regarding the type of democracy in Swaziland. The King introduced this concept to the nation the following morning at Mavuso Sports Centre in Manzini. Thousands of attendees were present, including diplomats, leaders of organs of state, governmental ministers, and civilians. The concept was "Monarchical Democracy," which is where the Kingdom and ballot box meet. This was a huge step for His Majesty whose desire was to bring balance between the Monarchy and the populace. One special aspect of that meeting was His Majesty handing over and sharing his podium with Dr. Myles Munroe. It was reportedly the first time he ever did that. This confirmed to us how fond His Majesty was of Myles Munroe. Indeed, eSwatini is one of those nations that Dr. Myles impacted and was scheduled to impact more. There were plans for Dr. Myles to train all spheres and levels of government of the nation in aspects of national leadership. It is part of our unfinished business that the Lord should help us continue to impact with Kingdom principles.

Royal Bafokeng Visit

It was a Friday night, October 17, 2014, when we arrived at the Royal Marang, the Royal Bafokeng nation's hotel where we stayed overnight. The next morning, the Queen Mother, Dr. Semane Molotlegi, came to the hotel and we had a briefing meeting with her. She was excited that

Dr. Myles would be the keynote speaker of the King Edward Patrick Lebone Molotlegi (Lebone I) Memorial Lecture, an annual event that former presidents and other prominent people have addressed. Dr. Myles spoke of the need to have visionary leadership if the nation were to prosper.

He also emphasized the need to not allow foreigners to take over the mineral resources of our nations. Of course, he highlighted the role of education in making a nation function. The Royal Bafokeng has a strong focus on youth education in safeguarding the future— not only for their nation but the country at large. Kgosi King Leruo Tshekedi Molotlegi was pleased with the message that Dr. Myles delivered at the lecture.

During this trip, Dr. Munroe adopted the Queen Mother as his mom since his mother had already passed. As a sign of her acceptance, the Queen Mother gave Dr. Myles a lion skin as a gift. I later presented it to the family at the funerals of Papa Myles and Mom Ruth in Nassau, Bahamas. The visit to the Royal Bafokeng opened a door of relationship which would last for years to come. In 2015, I took a trip there with Chairo and Charisa to introduce them to the King and Queen Mother. It was a great moment for both parties.

> My wife was due to give birth and Dr. Munroe said he would understand if I could not attend the conference. However, for some reason, Xoli urged and released me to go to the Bahamas. Dr. Munroe was excited about it, saying it was great that I could be there as I had my wife's blessing.

Tragedy Strikes

Dr. Myles and Mama Ruth had departed from Johannesburg, South Africa on October 31, 2014, after a month-long visit in Africa where I had hosted them and taken them on a six-nation tour.

The Global Leadership Forum was due to be held in the Bahamas in November 2014 and it is one I will never forget. My wife was due to give birth and Dr. Munroe said he would understand if I could not attend the conference. However, for some reason, Xoli urged and released me to go to the Bahamas. Dr. Munroe was excited about it, saying it was great that I could be there as I had my wife's blessing. After touching so many nations through the four visits to Africa that year, there was a lot for me to report, and so we were glad that my wife released me to go.

At the time, South African Airways (SAA) offered flights to either New York or Washington. If I chose New York then I could get a connecting flight to Nassau, Bahamas, where they lived. This meant we could attend church on Sunday morning, November 9, 2014, then travel on their jet to the conference which was held on another island called Freeport. However, the flights via New York were at inconvenient times and too expensive. I was forced to take the Washington flight, which got me to Freeport with only one stop. However, it meant I could not go to Nassau to join Dr. Myles and Mama Ruth. I had tried to find a way to travel to Nassau but just couldn't find a flight and finally gave up trying.

Bahamas Faith Ministries had a branch in Freeport and Dr. Munroe had taught there the previous year on the Sunday before the conference. This year he was going to start in Nassau and then come to Freeport on Sunday afternoon. The conference would then get underway on

Monday. I went to the morning service in Freeport but didn't enjoy it that day because my mind was in Nassau. I wanted to be with Dr. Munroe so badly, but it was just not meant to be. We were due to meet in Freeport around 6 p.m. I was looking forward to it as we had scheduled a welcome banquet with many of the international guests.

That year's Global Leadership Forum was set to be a special event. Andrew Young, who had marched with Martin Luther King Jr., was one of the speakers. He was also going to be honored at a pre-conference banquet where the other speakers would be introduced. Delegates usually begin arriving on Saturday ahead of the conference, which is held at the Royal Palm Resort in Freeport. Other guests flew in on Friday to enjoy a weekend of relaxation and sightseeing.

I was at the hotel after the church service when suddenly I heard people screaming and crying uncontrollably in the reception area and hallways of the hotel. It was obvious that something terrible must have happened and I tried to find out what it was. I came across my friend Eric Mabuza who indicated that Charisa was looking for me and she was crying. Some of the delegates informed me that Dr. Munroe's aircraft had been involved in an accident, but they did not know any details yet. One of the pastors at the church, Patrick Rolle, was in contact with the Bahamian Aviation Authorities but they were yet to release an official statement. We had no choice but to wait until 8 p.m. when they would share more details. That was a very heavy moment. A sense of foreboding filled the hotel. When they said there had been an accident, it was unthinkable to me that Myles Munroe could no longer be alive. I expected him to arrive and say he had a few bruises here and there but was otherwise alright. My head was spinning that night. I never imagined that the next news I heard would be so devastating. I didn't think I would ever hear such news again in my lifetime. It was a terrible, terrible moment. It was a moment of extreme disappointment, anger, and questioning God.

I was the closest to Dr. Munroe's son and daughter. They were at the hotel, but I could not face them. Pastor Rolle returned with the Minister of Transportation and other government officials to make the dreaded announcement. Dr. Munroe had sent an SMS saying the weather was bad and they were trying to circle. They hadn't been able to land but would be landing soon. We never heard from him again.

We were numb with shock but still had to decide whether the conference should go ahead. And if we continued with it, what form would it take? I was among those who said we should allow the conference to happen because Dr. Myles Munroe would have wanted it that way. It would also give us the chance to plan the way forward.

We finished our crisis meeting in the Bahamas around midnight. CNN broke the story that Dr. Myles Munroe had died in a plane crash, along with eight others. There were no survivors. They showed photos that he had posted on Facebook from one of our Africa trips. There were pictures of Dr. Munroe's jet along with an image of him and me in the jet. Another picture showed nine people posing together. They reported that his daughter Charisa had been on the plane. They probably talked to someone who said Charisa must have been there because she would have gone home first and then come with them. I remember being on the phone all night, pacing the floor of my hotel room, and fielding interviews from different media houses, print, radio, and television stations. At the same time, I was trying to come to terms with the loss. I hadn't yet seen his son and daughter.

A South African friend of ours, Werner Gruner, was working at one of the top banks in the Bahamas. He called my wife in tears after seeing the CNN report because he believed I had been on board the plane. My wife was a bit confused by this but told him I was already in Freeport and had not been in Nassau. Many of our friends gathered at my house in South Africa that Monday morning, November 10, because they also thought I was one of those who had crashed. They came to offer my wife their support and condolences. It was dark and gloomy in Freeport that Monday morning and the sun only came out around 8.30 a.m. I went to the conference in the same clothes I had worn the previous day. There hadn't been time to take a shower. It was just confusion all around. I was still fielding questions from the South African media: SAFM, 702, SABC, Phalaphala FM, another radio station in North West. Many of them knew Dr. Myles Munroe and me because we did interviews with media houses whenever he was on the continent of Africa. They knew who to talk to, so they kept me busy all day long.

The accident occurred when Dr. Myles's plane was approaching Grand Bahama International Airport, Freeport. I know that Dr. Munroe would never have forced the pilot to land. If he knew the weather was bad, it didn't matter whether a president was waiting for him on the ground, he would always take his cue from the captain when it came to flight safety. Secondly, the captain, Stanley Thurston, was a highly competent pilot with decades of experience. He had flown in all kinds of weather and didn't take chances. I had flown with him many times before without incident. I recall a conversation I once had with him about aviation. He described the refresher courses he regularly attended where they would learn about the different kinds of possible accidents and how to avoid them. Pilots learned how to control the aircraft in different conditions like crosswinds and emergency landings. He was a very well- trained pilot. I still don't know how this accident could have happened.

The newspapers dubbed the accident "Bahamas 911," referring to events that occurred on the same date in 2001 in the USA. I'm still praying and hoping that further information will emerge about the real cause of the Bahamas accident. There were nine people aboard the Learjet— Dr. Myles Munroe and his wife, Ruth, BFMI Senior Pastor, Dr. Richard Pinder, the pilot, Captain Stanley Thurston, First Officer Frahkan Cooper, newly-ordained youth pastors, Lavard Parks, his pregnant wife, Radel, and their five-year-old son, Johanan. One of Dr. Munroe's mentees, an American citizen named Diego DeSantiago, was also onboard. There were ten lives lost that fateful day, including the unborn baby. Dr. Munroe was sixty years old. We had celebrated his sixtieth birthday on April 20, 2014, and again in Sandton, Johannesburg, in August 2014. He passed away just three months after the Johannesburg, South Africa, party my office had organized.

The official accident report[1] revealed that rain and bad weather conditions had forced the plane, a Learjet 35A, registration number N17UF, to make a missed approach on its first attempt to land and go into a holding pattern at Grand Bahama International Airport in Freeport. The plane struck a harbor crane on its second approach at 4:52 p.m.

The flight plan for the trip from Lynden Pindling International Airport, Nassau, to Grand Bahama International Airport, Freeport, indicated a planned flight time of 24 minutes. This means that the aircraft had to circle the airport in Freeport for about twenty minutes. Bad weather conditions indeed. The pilot was trying to visually locate the runway when Air Traffic Control warned that conditions had deteriorated again. The report found that the plane had strayed well below its required minimum altitude on the approach, which placed it on a collision course with cranes at Freeport harbor.

Seeing Myles Jr. and Charisa for the first time after the accident was unbearable. When I walked into their hotel suite, we just cried and hugged one another for at least an hour. They realized that I was just as devastated as they were. Myles Jr. still reminds me today that when he saw me the pain only got worse. All I could say was, "I'm sorry, I'm sorry, I'm sorry…" I just didn't know what to say. It was a difficult and heavy moment and a season that would last for years.

Dr. Myles and Mom Ruth would have stayed in the same executive suite. It had several rooms and was luxurious and spacious enough to receive visitors. The then Prime Minister of the Bahamas, The Right Honorable Perry Christie, came there and spoke to us after he visited the crash site. However, I only went to the crash site with the university professor and author, and one of Dr. Myles Munroe's spiritual fathers, Dr. Jerry Horner, and several others after we concluded the conference.

The Global Leadership Forum normally ran from Monday to Thursday. This time it ended on Wednesday to allow time to cool off and get into preparations. I went to the crash scene on Thursday. It was a moment of harsh reality for me, and I was once again overwhelmed by disappointment and anger, and full of questions that only God could answer. By the time we arrived there, officials had already taken away the bodies and removed some of the debris. There were still a few pieces of the aircraft and personal belongings lying about. I saw somebody's jacket, a tie, and a shoe which didn't belong to either Dr. Munroe or Dr. Pinder. There was also a clicker, which we concluded belonged to Diego DeSantiago. The impact with the crane tore off the outer section of the aircraft's right wing. This sent the plane spinning out of control until it crashed inverted into a shipyard. The fuselage struck a

> Seeing Myles Jr. and Charisa for the first time after the accident was unbearable. When I walked into their hotel suite, we just cried and hugged one another for at least an hour. They realized that I was just as devastated as they were.

generator housing and caused extensive damage. It was clear that this was not a survivable accident. It happened suddenly and I believe they never knew what hit them. The final crash site was not far from the crane and so it must have only taken several seconds to impact the ground.

I suggested to Myles Jr. that he obtain pieces of the wreckage if possible. They could convert Dr. Myles and mom Ruth Munroe's house into a museum as part of plans to preserve their legacy. In 2015, we were able to establish the Myles and Ruth Munroe Foundation which is serving as an extension of the work of Dr. Myles and Mama Ruth Munroe. Charisa lives in the USA. She got a job there after leaving school and became a US citizen. Myles Jr. lives in the Bahamas, and it has been a pleasure working with both Charisa and Myles Jr. even after the departure of both Dr. Myles and Mama Ruth. The family home has remained unoccupied since the accident, although there is a housekeeper who comes in from time to time.

As you can imagine, this event in our lives has been very traumatic. I still haven't gotten over it and it will take years to come to terms with it. Dr. Munroe meant everything to me. I had mentioned and typed his name every day of my life.

Returning to South Africa after that conference was exceedingly difficult. I had to come back here and face my wife, administrator, and PA at the office. What could I possibly say to them? How would we recover from this? What did the future hold? It was an incredibly sad story and moment for us as an organization. But I know one thing—Dr. Myles Munroe would have wanted us to continue living out God's purpose for our lives and reach our potential. And with God's help, we are going to do exactly that.

A Sad Farewell

After the conference in Freeport, I flew to Nassau to give my support to Myles Jr. and Charisa Munroe, as well as the Pinder family. They were all going through so much, given the grief they were feeling and at the same time being busy with the funeral preparations.

It took me time to realize that it was not just Dr. Myles who had passed on but also Mama Ruth, Dr. Pinder, and six others. This was all just mind-blowing and unfathomable. I remember the evening of November 14, 2014, like it was yesterday. Myles Jr. took me to the family house in Yorkshire Street where Dr. Myles and Mama Ruth had lived. The house felt very empty in their absence. Myles Jr. called me to join him in the main bedroom and led me to Dr. Myles's closet. He asked me to take as many ties as I wanted. I chose ten ties I knew Dr. Myles liked. I still cherish and treasure them today.

I was honored to drive around with Myles Munroe Jr. as he had meetings at funeral homes and went to banks. I was also honored to help him with the process of selecting and buying a plot for their grave site.

It was a long trip back to South Africa. During the eighteen hours of flights, I was still filled with a sense of grief and hopelessness. I could not imagine how life was going to be without my Commander-in-Chief, Dr. Myles Munroe. I was not too sure he had completed his assignment on earth. I recall what Dr. Myles had said about death and dying and I realized in many ways he had prepared us for this eventuality over the years. I thought about his teachings on Purpose, Leadership, and Vision beyond the Visionary. The book he wrote called Passing It On had suddenly become even more relevant. I realized that Dr. Myles had done much preparation for his departure from the planet.

I recalled the recent Six Nations Kingdom Leadership tour. Although Dr. Myles Munroe was generally a people person, something extra-special marked that tour in October 2014. He asked to take photos with almost everyone, including random persons he suspected knew him. He was a happy man on that trip. On the same tour, the President of Burundi, the late Honorable Pierre Nkurunziza, invited Dr. Munroe to have dinner with him. Top government leaders, including cabinet members and ministers, attended the meeting. However, we were unaware of the deep relationship the president had with God. Upon arrival, protocol personnel received us and ushered us through security. As we arrived at the State House, we heard the sound of gospel music and discovered that the Honorable President was running the service and leading praise and worship! Imagine the president of your country dancing and sweating and praising the Lord. He later told us that they hold a weekly service at State House to thank God for another week of safety. He related how he had once spent weeks in the bush injured during the fight in the liberation struggle before he became president. It was during those weeks of his stay in the bush where he had met the Lord and vowed to praise and worship him if he would spare his life. He also told us the worship band members and singers were his bodyguards! It was clear that he was a man of Word, Worship, and Prayer. When the worship session ended, Dr. Munroe taught about Righteous Government. The attendees were truly edified and challenged. Both President Nkurunziza and Dr. Munroe were happy to meet for the first time and connected at a deeper level as kindred spirits.

> Dr. Myles had taught about death and mentioned a few times that he would not die before he had accomplished his purpose. He wanted people to rejoice at his funeral, not dress in black but wear bright colors.

After that service, we had a time of fellowship with Dr. Myles and the president exchanging ideas on aspects of leadership. As usual, Dr. Myles dominated the discussion. It was the first time I saw Myles Munroe that excited in the presence of a Head of State. I just knew something special had taken place in his heart.

When we arrived back at the hotel, Dr. Myles asked our group—me, Mandla Mvelase, Eric Rakumakwe, Felicia Rakumakwe, Makalo Mulidzwi, and Eugene Masebe Singo—to sit with him in the reception area. He took a seat on a couch and rested his feet on a footstool. We all sat around him and listened intently to what he would say.

Dr. Myles said that he had finally seen what he had been longing to see—a worshipping king. He explained that his desire had always been to see a King who knew the King of Kings. He said that he could now rest and that myself, Mandla, and the other mentees could take it from there. Dr. Myles spoke about that for the rest of the trip. He even highlighted that incident the first Sunday he returned to the Bahamas at the Bahamas Faith Ministries service on November 9 th , a few hours before the crash.

Dr. Myles had taught about death and mentioned a few times that he would not die before he had accomplished his purpose. He wanted people to rejoice at his funeral and not dress in black but wear bright colors. This is because death had no power or sting. After all, he lived righteously and did not live in sin. That is how I knew that his job was done when he died. Dr. Myles had written what he was meant to write, taught all he had to teach, and prepared leaders in all his organizations. These recollections and many more helped me to get to grips with his passing. It did not reduce the pain but did expand my understanding.

The trip back to South Africa was filled with memories and reflections of our lifetime together, and what life after the Munroes was to look like. Arriving home, I began organizing the five memorial services we were to have in the different regions on the African continent. These memorial services were held from November 15 - 29, 2014, as we needed to travel back by November 30, 2014. We were able to conduct the following memorial services: CRC, Pretoria (Pastor At Boshoff); New Covenant Fellowship, Redhill, Durban (Dr. Basil & Ma Anne Tryon); Turning Point Church, White River, Nelspruit (Pastor Nigross Manana); Manna Tabernacle, Polokwane, Limpopo (Dr. Strike Manganyi); The Purpose Centre Church, Nairobi, Kenya (Pastor Julian Kyula); Greater Love Ministries, Windhoek, Namibia (Pastor Haruna Goroh).

Many other memorial services were conducted across the continent of Africa and around the world. The memorial services were a huge success and we experienced love and comfort from people who deeply loved Dr. Myles Munroe and Mama Ruth. Government leaders, politicians, and business leaders were among those who attended the different memorial services. After conducting all the memorial services, we were exhausted but still had to travel to the Bahamas on November 30 for the funerals of Dr. Myles & Mama Ruth scheduled for December 4, 2014. My wife had just given birth on November 1, but she had to travel with me to the Bahamas, leaving our less than a month old Andisa under the care of my mom and the nanny. In honor of Mama Ruth, we named our daughter Andisa Makaria Ruth. Makaria is the name her godmother Charisa Munroe gave her.

Our early arrival in Nassau, Bahamas, on December 1, ensured we could attend the funeral of Dr. Richard Pinder (Vice-President of Bahamas Faith Ministries) on December 3. He was among those whose lives were claimed in the aircraft accident. This was a very dark, sad, and gloomy moment for all of us who knew them. Arriving in the Bahamas, I accompanied Myles Jr. and Charisa as they ran errands in preparation for the joint funeral service of both Dr. Myles and Mama Ruth.

One of the heaviest moments was when Myles Jr. and Charisa asked me and Xoli to speak at the funeral. We were to speak as the best friends of Dr. Myles and Mama Ruth Munroe. It was an absolute honor for both of us to share the platform as we gave tribute to the Kingdom couple who made us who we became.

A Tribute to Dr. Myles and Mama Ruth Ann Munroe
(Charlie Masala's speech at the joint funeral service)
Thursday, December 4, 2014, Nassau, Bahamas

There are no intelligible words to describe the feeling of deep hurt from the sudden recall of our parents and mentors, Dr. Myles & Ruth Munroe, together with a team that was on the private jet with them on Sunday, November 9th, 2014, in Freeport, Grand Bahama.

I got to know Dr. Myles Munroe through Trinity Broadcasting Network in 1990 after his message on purpose at Azusa in Tulsa, Oklahoma. My path crossed with Dr. Myles Munroe and his dear wife, Mama Ruth, in 1993, and in October 1995, I was part of a team of college students that invited him to address 6000 of us students at Technikon Northern Transvaal in Pretoria, South Africa. After the sessions, he accepted without hesitation my request that he be my mentor; he went further to meet my parents in Limpopo, over 400 kilometers away. Papa Myles called me "His special African son." Papa Myles always said that God had him in mind when he created me.

In July 1997, I made my first trip to the Bahamas at his invitation and have made these yearly trips without fail ever since. My wife, Xoli, and I virtually became their son and daughter, while we also dedicated ourselves to running their Africa Office and programs, putting in abeyance our prosperous Management Consulting business. We have been honored to assist them to take the message of the Kingdom to earthly kings, queens, Heads of State, governments, business executives, pastors, and the young and old in many African countries. In all this, we witnessed their love for African people, young or old, rich or poor, Christian or non- Christian, thus giving credence to Dr. Munroe's motto: "You must reduce everyone to a human, made in the image of God." Papa Myles loved people and if you were not careful, you would think you were the only person Dr. Munroe loved.

Papa was the same person, both onstage and off. He could participate in any discussion on any societal matter, showing the capacity to know something about everything. Dr. Munroe honored authorities, but he was not afraid to speak the truth to power. Africa had a special place in the hearts of Papa and Mama, so much so that they spent more time on the continent in their last years than anywhere else. Papa and Mama were so genuine and exemplary a couple that they challenged many couples to live up to the highest standards of marriage. They also showed that one can be diligent and work hard while simultaneously maintaining a stable and happy family. We believe that they lived their purpose to the full and we owe them a responsibility to take forward the legacy so well accomplished.

What we ponder flows from the people they were, the lives they impacted, and the example they gave us. God honored us and all of humanity with these special gifts, who not only taught and led but demonstrated a life of integrity, justice, and righteousness, thereby leaving us a clear example to follow. They could make others feel special and transformed us through the power of words. They committed to unleashing the leader trapped within us. They invested in teaching us.

Some of the lessons that come to mind include the following:

Embrace life as a mystery in its manifold forms. In life, there are questions you cannot answer, things you cannot explain, things you cannot change, things you cannot stop, things you cannot control, things you cannot go beyond, and things you are not responsible for. Embrace that mystery from the book, Rediscovering Kingdom Faith.

Your value in life is not in its duration but its donation. Investing in people keeps you alive beyond your grave.

If what you learn, accomplish, and accumulate dies with you, then you are a generational failure. As he said, the greatest act of leadership is what happens in your absence. He went on to say,"Success without a successor is a failure." True leaders invest in people. Indeed, he invested in us, and we will continue to invest in others.

Papa Myles loved his country, the Bahamas, so much that he even convinced God to move His residential address there from Africa!

He called the Bahamas *"The Place Where God Lives."* That statement protected the Bahamas over the years.

As **Philippians 4** and **verse 9** says, *"Whatever you have learned or received or heard from me, or seen in me—put it into practice. And the God of peace will be with you."*

As sons and mentees, let us take the baton and mantle of being new vessels of the vision.

We **commit that we shall keep alive their legacy** and take it to greater heights. The memory of the righteous is a blessing.

We **commit to dying empty.** They said all they had to say, wrote all they had to write, and worked all they had to work, now in glory as faithful servants!

Romans 14 and **verses 7 through 8 says**, "For not one of us lives for himself, and not one dies for himself; for if we live, we live for the Lord, or if we die, we die for the Lord; therefore whether we live or die, we are the Lord's."

I am comforted to know that death has no power over you, and it can't sting you for you didn't live in sin.

Goodbye, our hero and heroine, the Moses of Africa and the Third World. Hambani kahle qhawe ne qhawekazi. Vha tshimbile zwavhudi. Fambani kahle. Tsamaya hanhle. Mooi loop. Journey well! Africa loves you, and your work will continue to yield fruit for a better Africa, the Bahamas, and the world.

Mr. Charlie Masala: South Africa
CEO: Myles Munroe International-Africa,
Senior Vice President: International Third World Leaders Association

A Tribute to Mama Ruth Ann Munroe
(Mrs. Xoli Masala's speech at the joint funeral service)
Thursday, December 4, 2014, Nassau, Bahamas

Fifteen years ago, I met a beautiful, warm-hearted, humble, and immaculate, yet very intelligent woman of God filled with wisdom. Your inner beauty and kindness resembled a full moon in the still of the night. You were a Kingdom ambassador who lived by truth delivering guidance selflessly.

I'm yet to meet such a soul more than a mother to us. You were a sister, a girlfriend, and everything else a married woman could ever need and ask for. With a soft voice and gentler spirit, you only spoke when there was a need to say something, which was very humbling for me, knowing you were married to Papa, who was such an eloquent and outspoken man. Followers would often come and take Papa away from you almost oblivious to your presence, but you remained poised, unperturbed, and embraced everyone. You always looked elegant and on point, your beauty worn and radiated from within.

Your teachings will always be the food for my soul and the calm voice in my mind. You taught and showed me to respect and honor my husband, be his cheerleader, raise my hands in covering him, kneel in prayer for him, and always meet his needs. Mama, there are a lot of things I have learned and done with you, and I cherish them all. I thank God, our King of Kings, who made our paths meet and become an integral part of each other's lives. You taught us, we learned, and now that you are resting in the bosom of our Lord the Creator with Papa by your side. It is time for us to take on the candle, continue your work of empowering others with knowledge about the word of God, and light the world with love.

I am going to miss you dearly…the long flights and trips that we took together, the shopping, the hearty laughter at the end of a long, busy day, and the midnight snacks at the hotels where we stayed. I remember we used to eat French fries and dip them in mayonnaise and tomato sauce. I remember the faces of onlookers, filled with bemusement at what we were doing. Ah! Such memories I will treasure.

You introduced us to your beautiful children, Charisa and Chairo They will forever be our younger sister and brother—and rest assured we will take care of them always. It is difficult for me to accept that you have been called to your final home. I am extremely saddened and shocked by your passing; however, I know the Lord will make a way for me to heal. I love you Mama, and I miss you. Although there is pain, I'm at peace knowing that you are with the Lord, and I'll see you again, when my time to come home arrives. You were wonderful, loved, and treated me like a daughter, and I loved and honored you as a mother. I'll miss your voice, our phone conversations, and our prayer times. You'll always be in my thoughts, and you will hold a special place in my heart.

The last day I spoke to you over the phone, you said to me, "Our beautiful daughter, we love and we pray that you have a good delivery and thank you for doing the will of God!" Those we love don't go away. They walk beside us every day...unseen, unheard, but always near...still loved, still missed, and very dear.

Your loving daughter.

Mrs. Xoli Masala: South Africa
Myles Munroe International-Africa

Charlie with his siblings in the early days

This is one of the first photos taken of Dr. Myles Munroe and Charlie Masala, 1995

Dr. Myles Munroe and Charlie Masala at Dr. Myles' home in 2004

Dr. Myles Munroe singing at the Technikon Northern Transvaal, 1995

The Munroe Family: Myles Jr (Chairo), Charisa, Mama Ruth and Papa Myles

89

Charlie, Mama Ruth & Dr. Myles presented with a leadership award in 2014

Trip to Uganda, 2014

Dr. Myles and Charlie travelling to Miramar, Florida, 2012, and to Eswatini (Swaziland) in 2012

MMI Africa Volunteers

Mama Ruth Munroe with Xoli Masala at Choose Life Church, Pretoria East, 2011

Dr. Myles speaking at Choose Life Church, for Ps. John, Mandri and Aunty Pal Roebert

Dr. Myles ministering a word to Ps. John Roebert at Choose Life Church, 2013

Dr. Myles at Jesus Calls Ministries in Swaziland with the Ripley family, 2013

Dr. Myles with Media Personality Tami Ngubeni, 2013

Dr. Myles with Bishop Mosa and Ps. Gege Sono, Grace Bible Church, 2013

Dr. Myles meets President Nelson Mandela

Dr. Myles Munroe with Royal Bafokeng nKgosi (King) Leruo Molotlegi in Phokeng, Rustenburg

Dr. Myles and Mama Ruth with the Queen Mother of Royal Bafokeng, Mmemogolo

91

Dr. Myles with Dr. Basil Tryon praying for the Khoisan King

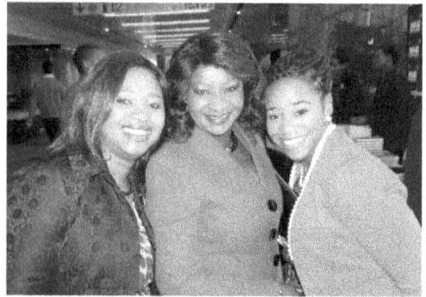

Xoli and Charisa with Mama Ruth Munroe at the welcome dinner in 2014

Dr. Myles Munroe with his son Myles Jr. at the ITWLA Forum in 2013

Conference at Emperors Palace in Johannesburg, 2007

A proud moment

Charlie and Myles Munroe Jr.

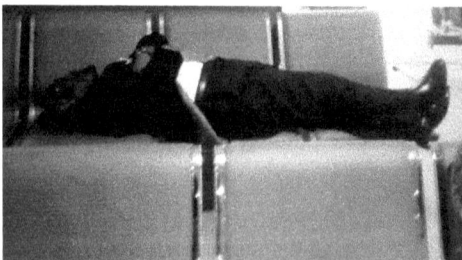

Dr. Myles resting on a bench at King Shaka Airport, Durban, after teaching at New Covenant Fellowship

Book signing in Gabon, 2014

Dr. Myles and Mama Ruth in
Jerusalem, Israel, in 2011

Charlie and Xoli with Myles Jr. and Charisa
in Jerusalem, Israel

Xoli Masala with Charisa and Myles Jr. at
Myles and Ruth Munroe lecture, 2015

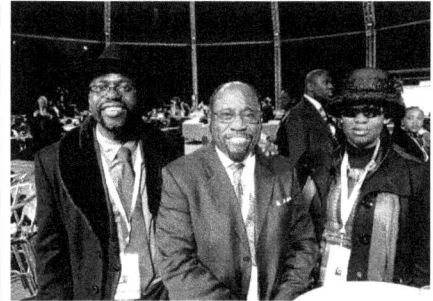

Dr. Myles with Prof. Tshilidz Marwala and a
guest at Presidential Inauguration in 2014

Dr. Myles and Mama Ruth on a wildlife excursion in South Africa

Charlie's dad, Wilson, and his mom, Shandukani Masala, with Myles Jr.

Dr. Myles & Mama Ruth with Mr. Ripley, Dr. Alex and Ma Busi Tsela, Eric and Mpumi Mabuza

Dr. Myles and Mama Ruth with Ps. At Boshoff and CRC Family, Bloemfontein

Charlie and Xoli Masala attending Bahamas Faith Ministries in Nassau, Bahamas, 2015

Charlie Masala teaching as part of a panel at a meeting in Nassau, Bahamas

Charlie with the Ripleys in Atlanta

Charlie with Bishop Carlton Pearson at Oral Roberts University in 2015

Dr. Myles with Charlie, Xoli and the Masala
Children in 2014

Dr. Myles with the current
President Cyril Ramaphosa

Reports of the plane crash

Photos of the crash site

Remembering our loved ones and celebrating their lives

Memorial and Funeral Service for Drs. Myles and Ruth Munroe

Funeral and Memorial Service

Charlie and Xoli welcoming Myles Jr. at the O.R. Tambo Airport in Johannesburg, South Africa with Remembrance T-shirts, 2015

Myles Jr. and Charlie plant a tree at the Jordan River, Israel, 2015, in honor of Dr. Myles and Ruth Munroe

Dr. Myles Munroe's Legacy Lives On – Article in Joy! Magazine, South Africa, Feb 2022

PART 3

MYLES MUNROE'S IMPACT ON NATIONS IN AFRICA & OTHER THIRD WORLD / DEVELOPING NATIONS

Without a doubt, the name of Myles Munroe can be placed high among those in history who have had a tremendous impact on the world. Former Prime Minister of the Bahamas, Perry Christie, said of him, "He was a towering force who earned the respect and admiration not only of Christian adherents but of secular leaders both here at home and around the world."[2] Saddened after the news of Munroe's tragic plane crash, Christie called the loss, "Utterly impossible to measure." Although Myles Munroe is no longer with us, his wisdom and presence are still felt in the lives of individuals and nations he touched, particularly in Africa and the Caribbean. In this section, I have included media reports of Myles Munroe's visits to developing nations to provide a different perspective on his ministry at the highest levels of government.

Impact on South Africa (multiple visits between 1990 and 2014)

South Africa was a hub country on the African continent for Dr. Myles Munroe's work from 1991 onwards. If there was a country that Dr. Myles and Mama Ruth loved and even said they could live in, it was South Africa. The Bahamas and South Africa always shared a great relationship since our founding fathers, Nelson R. Mandela, Robert Mugabe, and Sir Lynden Oscar Pindling were friends as they studied some law programs together in England back in the younger days. After completing these programs, Pindling became Prime Minister of the Bahamas, Mugabe became President of Zimbabwe, and Mandela returned to South Africa but became president after spending 27 years in prison.

The Commonwealth Heads of Government Meeting 1985 (CHOGM) was the eighth Meeting of the Heads of Government of the Commonwealth of Nations. It was held in Nassau, The Bahamas, between October 16, 1985, and October 22, 1985, and hosted by that country's Prime Minister, Sir Lynden Pindling. The Nassau Accord called on the government of South Africa to dismantle its apartheid policy, enter negotiations with the country's Black majority, and end its occupation of Namibia. The Commonwealth Eminent Persons Group was appointed to investigate the South African issue and report back with recommendations ahead of the special 1986 CHOGM in London.

Following his release from prison, Nelson Mandela visited the Bahamas and thanked Sir Lynden Pindling for his role in opposing apartheid. It is through this relationship that Dr. Myles Munroe met Mandela during the latter's visit to Nassau, Bahamas. As someone who was also dedicated to addressing the evils of apartheid, Dr. Myles impacted all sectors of society in South Africa—government, politics, business, academia, and the church. Myles Munroe will remain a household name in South Africa for a long time.[3]

He was particularly concerned about the inequality in land owner-ship in South Africa, even after twenty years of freedom and majority rule. Dr. Myles had opportunities to meet and train senior leaders in South African politics, government, business, and the church. He is un-doubtedly one of those foreign global leaders who helped to change the mindsets of both oppressed and oppressor, as we moved from apartheid rule to democracy. His input to the nation was vital and will never be ignored. Dr. Munroe warned South Africa that the unresolved issue of land was a time bomb if left unaddressed and he felt that freedom was not complete without land and economic freedom.

Impact on Namibia (1998, 2013, 2014)

Dr. Myles Munroe's first visit to the southwest African nation of Na-mibia was in 1998. I remember joining him on that trip and watched as he addressed the Cabinet Ministers of the Republic of Namibia led by President Samuel Shafiishuma Daniel Nujoma and Prime Minister Hage G. Geingob. Both leaders loved Myles Munroe and the president even opened his residence to Dr. Myles and his team. Namibia, like many other countries, came from a history of colonial rule. Dr. Myles taught on creating a national vision and pursuing the dream of a prosperous nation for formerly oppressed citizens.

Dr. Myles visited a poor area just outside of Windhoek and was touched by the poverty. I remember him reaching out to the children who were surrounded by flies, and he hugged them and prayed for them. That was just one of the few incidents where I saw him weep like that. Dr. Myles advised and challenged the government of Namibia to expropriate land and get the land back to government ownership so they could redistribute it to the Namibians. He explained that there is no freedom without land. It was made clear to him that most of the land was in the hands of a few people and families who had no vested interest in the development of the Namibians.

Dr. Myles returned to Namibia again in 2013 and 2014. He had opportunities to meet senior leaders in politics, government, business, and the church, and he was committed to helping bring a much-needed change to the country. Munroe poured out everything he had to make an impact, and he encouraged his followers to "die empty." Many Namibian leaders followed his leadership. He meant so much to the nation and the people. His principles live on in this nation. People attended his sessions regardless of what day of the week the sessions were held. Dr. Myles challenged the church not to remain passive but to get involved in ushering in a "new Namibia."

After the shocking and unexpected passing of Dr. Myles and mom Ruth Munroe, Pastor Haruna Goroh of Greater Love Ministries (who usually hosted Dr. Munroe in Namibia) told the media that he was still trying to come to terms with it. He said that Munroe had recently sent him a special message on the church's 20th anniversary and Goroh's wedding anniversary. They had planned to bring Dr. Munroe back to Namibia for many years to come. Pastor Goroh further said that Dr. Myles and Ruth Munroe's marriage was worth emulating, as they loved each other and stuck together as a couple.

Secretary-General of the Council of Churches of Namibia, Reverend Maria Kapere, said that Munroe taught leadership principles from a biblical perspective. As such, he had a holistic approach to how leaders in public office should conduct themselves.

Kapere said, "Without godly inspired leadership it is difficult for a leader to thrive in his or her position." She further explained that Munroe in his teachings also focused on the family, and he wanted the church to make an impact on families. This is because if a family is broken society becomes broken. His teachings were to influence the right approach to nation-building," Kapere said. Even though Dr. Myles didn't live long enough to see the implementation of the land program and reduction of poverty in Namibia, the seed he planted will surely germinate and yield much fruit.

Myles Munroe Visits Zimbabwe

Dr. Myles Munroe's first visit to Zimbabwe was in 1993 at the invitation of Archbishop Ezekiel Guti of ZAOGA Forward in Faith Ministries in Harare. Dr. Myles was the main speaker at the ZAOGA International Christian Leadership Summit attended by delegates from all over the world. Archbishop Guti was one of the first Trustees of the International Third World Leaders Association (ITWLA).

Dr. Myles respected Bishop Guti and always referred to him as his Papa. On that trip, Dr. Myles was given a diplomatic assignment by the Bahamian Prime Minister at the time, Sir Lynden Pindling to personally deliver to Zimbabwe president Robert Mugabe. Dr. Myles became increasingly concerned about the state of the economy, poverty, and unemployment, among many other challenges. Even in the early days, Dr. Munroe was already challenging leaders to think about the beneficiation of mineral and agricultural resources. At the leadership summit, he challenged native Zimbabweans to grow food, beneficiate their minerals, and develop finished products.

Myles Munroe Visits Botswana

> Myles Munroe said that Zambia needed more than peace to expand the economy and lift the population out of poverty through a vision-orientated leadership. Zambia needs wealth. Zambia needs visionary leadership.

In 2013, Dr. Myles visited the nation of Botswana for the first time. Bishop Frank Boago Ramogapi (Bishop Rams) of Royal Assembly Ministries hosted him.

We met former president, Sir Ketumile Quett Joni Masire, who was in office from 1980 to 1998. Dr. Munroe spoke on issues of developing a national vision at a conference which national leaders attended. He encouraged the people to learn from elders like Masire who was present at the meeting at a local hotel where the conference was held. Dr. Myles's message in Botswana leaned more towards Business Development to help grow the nation's economy and he also taught about Rediscovering the Kingdom of God.

Myles Munroe Visits Zambia

Dr. Myles visited Zambia twice in his lifetime, the first time in the mid-'90s when Fredrick Chiluba was President and again in 2013 when Michael Sata was President.

In October 2013, we were there when President Sata was on sick leave and said to be out of the country seeking medical assistance in England. We met his Vice-President at the time, Guy Lindsay Scott. Mr. Scott became the President of Zambia just a year after we visited Lusaka following the death of President Sata. Our meeting with Vice-President Scott took place in a holding room at the Convention Centre just before Dr. Myles addressed a packed venue of Zambian national leaders and captains of industry. Dr. Myles spoke on national leadership, developing a national vision, and corruption.

The media reported on the Friday night event, quoting the Bahamas-born, celebrated motivational speaker, preacher, and author, Myles Munroe, as saying that Zambia needed more than peace to expand the economy and lift the population out of poverty through a vision-oriented leadership. "Zambians can't eat peace. Peace is good but you can't eat peace. Zambia needs wealth. Zambia needs visionary leadership." Dr. Munroe advised the delegates that, instead of seeing obstacles everywhere, the Zambian leadership and people should "emulate the King of the Jungle, the lion, which, despite being small, conquers huge animals like elephants. When a lion sees an elephant, it says, 'There is my lunch.' It does not see something huge. Zambia should be like that. Its leadership should be like that."

Myles Munroe Visits Malawi

Dr. Myles Munroe: The Greatest Revolutionary. Let me admit that the first time I heard of the name Dr. Myles Munroe was two months ago. I heard his name from Calvary Family Church International officials who announced that Dr. Munroe would be in Malawi on October 21, 2012. And, today, I was privileged to be one of the people who went to welcome him at the Chileka International Airport in Blantyre around 10:00 a.m. this morning.

Dr. Munroe disembarked from his private jet, along with his wife Ruth, his daughter, his son, a niece, and Charlie Masala, among others. After disembarking from the plane, he headed for the V.I.P. lounge, where he shook the hands of each one of us before answering some questions. But it is not the antics of Chileka Airport I want to talk about. I want to talk about his "The Kingdom and the Church" sermon at Robin's Park in Blantyre an hour later. You can also call it the Calvary Kingdom Service of Worship. Dr. Munroe is simply a great orator who has changed my life forever today! The way he talked of dominion, colonialism, governance, and other issues…I am flabbergasted. I was especially enthralled with his statements that the terms "holy," "repent," and other stuff, are not religious. He then elaborated his statements with concrete examples.

Surely, as I left Robin's Park one hour ago, I felt the changes in my heart. It is like his spirit was speaking to mine. This afternoon, he will be speaking to various leaders at Robin's Park. Tomorrow, he goes.

Why does time pack all the goodies in briefs? Eish, before I forget. Munroe's first words upon arrival at Chileka International Airport were: "I am home!" He was serious. His tone was emotional. Dr. Munroe is home now. He is in Malawi, the Warm Heart of Africa. And, before I forget again, Dr. Munroe said something to the same effect (of being home) at Robin's Park at the onset of his sermon. He said: "It has taken me 259 years to set foot on home soil!" Yet the Bahamian inspirational speaker was born less than 259 years ago—on April 20, 1954—and is only aged 58. Dr. Munroe was talking of the vices of slavery and its twin brother of colonization: They made Africans so near (to each other, in spirit), yet so far away (in culture, language, belief system). Oh, the colonizers and slave masters and mistresses killed the mind of the great people of Africa! In these roles, he has crisscrossed the earth, drilling leaders in education, media, religion, sports, government administration, among others.

Today, speaking to Malawians who couldn't believe what they were hearing, nobody wondered why he is the founder of Bahamas Faith Ministries International (BFMI) and head of Myles Munroe International (MMI), which runs leadership training institutes, a publishing company, a missions agency, a television network, web communications, radio, and a church community.

Yes, nobody had any lingering doubts about why he is the chief executive officer and chairman of the board of the International Third World Leaders Association and president of the International Leadership Training Institute. Yes, everybody could finally understand why he is the author of 23 books and an inspiring speaker.

But Zachimalawi feels that he is more than that; he is the greatest revolutionary. He sets the mind free. He lets people think for themselves. He is a great man. Through slavery, which grabbed his ancestors from Africa, the motherland, those cruel savages took away our pride, our greatest minds. Through colonization, they arrested our free-thinking capabilities. They gave us their language, making us believe that theirs was the best language; they imposed their leadership style, sending us heartless governors whose only duty was to live and preach their kingdom's symbols abroad; they then killed our minds—through this corrupted education system that propagates what is in the best interest of the masters.

But Munroe comes in the morning, with the keys of the mind, and liberates us to the times that were—when free-thinking was the currency of productive life. This man. Dr. Myles Munroe![4]

Myles Munroe Visits Uganda

Dr. Myles Munroe only visited this East African country once but with great impact. Dr. Myles was well-liked in Uganda with the First Lady being his number one fan. In October 2013, Dr. Munroe made remarks at the 15th National Prayer Breakfast. In attendance was the President of Uganda Hon Yoweri Museveni held at Hotel Africana in Kampala.

The occasion was organized by Members of the Uganda Parliament under the theme "Advancing into the Next 50 Years with a National Vision." Dr. Munroe tackled the power of visionary leadership for National Development and said the greatest need in the 21st Century is visionary leadership for development to occur. While leading the closing prayer, Mrs. Janet Museveni, who was also the Minister for Karamoja and MP Ruhaama Constituency, prayed to God to provide Ugandans with vision, strengthen their faith, and instill in their hearts and the hearts of the people of Africa, the spirit of brotherhood. Mrs. Janet Museveni had earlier joined the Parliamentary choir to sing the "Amazing Grace" hymn. The 15th National Prayer Breakfast was attended by delegations from sixteen countries worldwide, Cabinet Ministers, Members of Parliament, and religious leaders of all denominations, among others.

Deputy Speaker of Parliament Jacob Oulanyah and Dr. James Magara (host) of Uganda Jubilee Network were among the dignitaries who attended the Business Forum, Serena Hotel, Kampala addressed by Dr. Myles a day after the National Leadership Breakfast.

According to Munroe, a globalized market affects businesses in terms of competition and speed. He, however, argues that this also presents opportunities for a wider market and lower tariffs. On managing crises, Munroe advises businesses to consider every challenge as an opportunity for innovation. In a rather candid tone, Munroe emphasizes that the Church and wealth creation should not be separated. "Poor people cannot tithe. Build the people and they will build the ministry," he states, adding that clerics must build "a church of businesspeople and lead by example."

The most recent memory of Dr. Munroe in the minds of many Ugandans is when he graced parliament's 15th annual National Prayer Breakfast as the guest speaker on October 8, 2013.

His address on leadership was delivered clearly, each word forming a building block of another. The first lady Janet Museveni was among the first leaders to send out a condolence message after the passing of both Dr. Myles and Mama Ruth Munroe. In a tweet, Mrs. Museveni said she was deeply saddened by the death of the international preacher and renowned author.

In a press statement, the Speaker of Parliament Rebecca Kadaga said she was honored that he could respond to her invitation at rather short notice. Ms. Kadaga added, "Dr. Munroe and his wife will forever be remembered for their work and teachings on leadership, the discovery of purpose, maximizing of potential, vision, individual and national transformation, and for coaching and mentoring many leaders from around the world." Legislators have also expressed shock at the death of the international Leader and Speaker. One of the organizers of the annual prayer breakfast, Benson Obua-Ogwal, at which Munroe was the keynote speaker last year, says the world has lost an important religious leader. Ogwal cites his preaching on good leadership as one of the key messages that Uganda should emulate.

Meanwhile, Dr. James Magara (main host of our visit), chairperson of the Jubilee organizing committee, has described him as an "irreplaceable leader." The head of the born-again community in Uganda, Dr. Joseph Serwadda, too has spoken out describing Dr. Myles as a key pillar in the church who did a lot in spreading the word of God through preaching and publications.

Born on April 20, 1954, Munroe was the author of 69 books and a motivational speaker whose teaching cut across leadership, philosophy, theology, human inter-relations, and contemporary politics.[5]

Myles Munroe Visits Kenya

Dr. Myles Munroe visited Nairobi, Kenya, on two occasions, the first in 2013 and again in 2014, both trips hosted by Pastor Julian Kyula.* The visits focused on Leadership, Business Development, and Rediscovering the Kingdom. It was on the second and last trip in 2014 where the well-circulated interview with Jeff Koinange was conducted and filmed.

"I want to challenge every Kenyan to go to the cemetery and disappoint the graveyard. Die like the Apostle Paul who said, 'I have finished my course, I have kept the faith and I have been poured out like a drink offering,'" he told the show's host, Jeff Koinange. "There is nothing left. I am ready to die. That's how I want to die because there is nothing else for me left to die. When you die, die like I am planning to die. Empty. It's finished," he added. [6]

He was in Kenya on his Tour of Africa where he was visiting nine countries to speak about leadership and change. While in Kenya, Dr. Munroe pointed out that Kenya's education system needed adjustment.

Myles Munroe was the author of 69 books and a motivational speaker whose teaching cut across leadership, philosophy, theology, human inter-relations, and contemporary politics.

ROSE FROM AN F STUDENT TO OWN A JET

Dr. Munroe, who was born in the Bahamas as the sixth born in a family of 11, lived in a wooden house with four big rocks to support the house above the ground. He rose from such a poor background to own a private jet.

It was on this trip where Dr. Myles and the team also visited the victims of the Westgate Mall shootings who were admitted to the different hospitals around Nairobi. Dr. Myles spoke to the victims as he motivated them and reminded them that they have a purpose to fulfill and prayed for them.

Myles Munroe Visits Burundi

Dr. Myles Munroe visited Burundi once from October 25 to 27, 2014. We were hosted by Eglise Vivante Burundi, a ministry led by Ps Edmond Kivuye. Dr. Myles spoke about Rediscovering the Kingdom. On this visit, we were able to touch the National Leadership, Church Leaders, and the Youth. The Leadership Summit was attended by the Honorable late President Pierre Nkurunziza, his cabinet ministers, captains of industry, and heads of governmental and non-governmental institutions.

Dr. Myles Munroe spent a day with these national leaders as he taught about leadership. We were then invited by His Excellency President Pierre Nkurunziza to visit The State House of Burundi where Dr. Myles was asked to teach the guests who were mainly the Burundi cabinet members, presidential staff, and presidential family. On that night, President Nkurunziza led the worship team and choir in worship.

Dr. Myles advised the president on many levels, and we ended the night on a high note. It was clear that the two leaders were planning to do much more towards developing the country of Burundi, which had until recently experienced several wars, civil wars, and civil unrests.

Myles Munroe Visits Democratic Republic of Congo (DRC)

The Democratic Republic of the Congo, also known as Congo-Kinshasa, DR Congo, the DROC, Congo or The Congo, and historically Zaire, is a country in Central Africa. It is the largest country in sub-Saharan Africa by area, the second-largest in all of Africa, and the 11th-largest in the world. It is said to be one of the richest countries in the world in its variety of natural resources.

Dr. Myles visited the Democratic Republic of the Congo twice in 2012 and 2013, hosted by Dr. Jose Muzingu, a pastor and leadership developer originally from the DRC but residing in Boston, USA. In 2012, Dr. Munroe did back-to-back sessions covering the subject of national leadership vision, business development, and church and Kingdom meetings. Foyer Des Aigles International and Empower Africa hosted the Congo Bahamas Investment Forum 2013 in Kinshasa on October 26 at the Fleuve Congo Hotel to promote trade opportunities between the Bahamas and the Democratic Republic of the Congo. Dr. Myles Munroe, together with banking and finance expert, Werner Gruner, spoke on what it takes to become a financial center and they touched on the challenges of today's banking system as well as what the solution is.

Through an invitation from the former Deputy President Azarias Ruberwa Manywa, we were able to visit his residence where Dr. Myles conducted an informal leadership consultative session with him. Many aspects of national importance were discussed given that he is also a Kingdom Citizen responsible for the National Leadership Breakfast which includes all sectors of national leadership. Dr. Myles was tipped to address the National Breakfast in 2015.

Myles Munroe Visits Republic of the Congo

Through the invitation of Mr. William Goma, Dr. Myles Munroe was able to impact Brazzaville, the capital of the Republic of the Congo. Dr. Myles was able to address the political leadership and church leadership at the local level.

The Minister of Communications hosted at the Summits. The Republic of the Congo was formerly part of the French colony of Equatorial Africa. It was established on November 28, 1958, and gained independence from France in 1960. It was a Marxist–Leninist state from 1969 to 1992, under the name People's Republic of the Congo. Also known as Congo-Brazzaville, the Congo Republic, the Congo, or simply Congo, it is not to be confused with the neighboring Democratic Republic of the Congo.

Myles Munroe Visits Gabon

Dr. Myles Munroe visited the country of Gabon once in October of 2014 hosted by the late Pastor Gaetan Piebi. Gabon is a central African country rich in natural resources. Located on the Atlantic Ocean, it borders Cameroon, Equatorial Guinea, and the Republic of Congo. It is sparsely populated, with about 2 million inhabitants. Forests cover 85% of its territory.

There was no convention center big enough to host the Summit with Dr. Munroe and they ended up hiring a marquee to ensure a decent venue for the guests and dignitaries. Even though the people speak French, they knew who Myles Munroe was. We spent two days in Gabon. I remember a mob of people excited to receive us on arrival at the airport. They also followed us at the airport on the night we departed, October 31, 2014, just eight days before Dr. Myles and Mama Ruth together with the seven other passengers passed on in the aircraft accident in Freeport, Grand Bahama.

Myles Munroe Visits Nigeria

There is no doubt that the country Dr. Myles Munroe visited the most on the African continent was South Africa. However, the second country he visited most in Africa was Nigeria, a nation of nearly 2 million people in the southeast of West Africa. Dr. Munroe was and still is a popular name in Nigeria. The people loved him and always attended his meetings in big numbers.

He mostly visited the two main cities, Abuja and Lagos. Dr. Myles was largely concerned about leadership, corruption, and lack of development. His first trip to Nigeria was in the mid/late '90s when President Obasanjo was still in power. Munroe recalled that when he arrived at the president's residence, Obasanjo had his book The Burden of Freedom and you could see it was marked up.

Dr. Myles Munroe was a guest in many conferences in Nigeria. He addressed banks, oil companies, technology companies, insurance companies, and church organizations. Nigeria was enriched with the wisdom and teachings of Dr. Myles.

Myles Munroe Visits Ghana

Dr. Myles Munroe first visited Ghana in 1997 and again in 2012, which was without a doubt the most impactful trip.

Dr. Myles Munroe Meets with Ghana President and Addresses Leaders on Economic Explosion in Ghana, West Africa

His Excellency Professor John Evans Atta Mills, the President of the Republic of Ghana met with Dr. Myles Munroe and his delegation this week and spoke of Ghana's spiritual commitment to God and the Biblical foundations and that's its future is in God's hands.[7]

World acclaimed Bahamian multi-gifted teacher, motivational speaker, leadership consultant, entrepreneur, businessman, and statesman, Dr. Myles Munroe said the oil find in Ghana makes the country one of the leading emerging Third World countries at a time when First World countries were experiencing a consistent financial meltdown.

Dr. Munroe and his wife Ruth were welcomed to Accra, the capital of Ghana, Accra, by the Vice President of the Republic of Ghana, His Excellency Hon. John Dramani Mahama, Hon. E.T. Mensah, Minister of Water Resources, Works, and Housing, and Vice President Chief of Staff K.S. Baffoe Bonnie. Accompanying Dr. Munroe to Ghana on this official leadership Training tour were Mrs. Ruth Munroe, Dr. Peter Morgan, President of the International Third World Leaders Association (ITWLA), Vice President of ITWLA, Mr. Charlie Masala, and ITWLA member, Miss Celia Collins.

Dr. Munroe was hosted by Dr. Kingsley Fletcher, a longtime member of the Board of Trustees of ITWLA. "Dr. Munroe and your delegation, you are all welcome back home to your roots here in Ghana and we look forward to this launching the beginning of official relations with our Bahamian Family, especially those of the diaspora," said the

> Dr. Munroe was already impressed with the massive physical infrastructure he saw in Ghana, adding that the people of the Bahamas considered Ghana as their roots, so he was happy to return with good news.

Vice President. Dr. Munroe thanked the Vice President and the Government of Ghana for the warm reception and introduced his party of ITWLA delegates to the Vice President. "These are times when it is okay to be a Third World country because the first and second worlds are melting down while there is an explosion of new opportunities in the Third World countries and Ghana is one of those countries poised to experience economic explosion and assume a leadership role in Africa," he said.

Dr. Munroe was speaking at a press conference at the beginning of his five-day visit to Ghana to hold business leadership seminars for present and aspiring business leaders in Ghana, and to meet with top politicians, including President John Evans Atta Mills and other leaders. Dr. Munroe's team consists of Mrs. Ruth Munroe, Dr. Peter Morgan, President of the International Third World Leaders Association (ITWLA), Mr. Charlie Masala, Vice President of ITWLA. The visit was at the invitation of the renowned Ghanaian international pastor, leader, consultant, diplomat, statesman, and businessman, Dr. Kingsley Fletcher, and it is being facilitated by Sparrow International. It was designed to tap into the expertise, years of experience, and deep knowledge of Dr. Myles Munroe on business, Christianity, community, international and political leadership devoid of corruption, and characterized by integrity, and how that could drive economic development in Ghana.

The highlights of the visit were the Achievers Power Dinner held on Friday, March 2, 2012, at the Accra International Conference Centre with business leaders, where over 1000 leaders attended two sessions of training with Dr. Munroe, and the Aspirers Power Breakfast on Saturday, March 3, 2012, at the same venue, where the 1000 aspiring youth leaders were motivated to achieve their leadership potential.

Dr. Munroe said this was the first time in 15 years since he last visited Ghana and he was already impressed with the massive physical infrastructure he had seen in Ghana so far, adding that the people of the Bahamas considered Ghana as their roots, so he was happy to return to Ghana with the good news that "things are going to get better in Ghana soon." He said it was important to understand that in the scheme of global events where the economies of First World countries were breaking down, it was important to note that Africa was not part of the banking system of the First World so Africa would emerge when the First World falls. "The future belongs to the emerging economies and Ghana is one of them and perhaps that is why you have begun to tap into (oil and gas) resources which have been hidden for thousands of years until now. It is no coincidence that Ghana discovered oil at a time when the West is falling – this is because Ghana is destined to be a leader in the emerging world," he said. He predicted that the explosion of opportunities that have begun in Ghana would attract thousands of real foreign direct investments into Ghana, adding that he was personally going to champion investments from the Bahamas and other parts of the world into Ghana. "I reach millions of people with my television programs across the world, and I am going to use that platform to project the tourism and investment opportunities in Ghana and drive investors into the country," he said.

Dr. Munroe noted that Ghana's thriving democracy, characterized by at least two smooth transitions of change of power was a plus to the country because it assured investors of political, economic, and social stability. He, however, noted that without a solid, strong, competent, and well- grounded leadership, no nation or organization could experience and sustain any meaningful development. Dr. Munroe said the oil find puts Ghana on the verge of becoming a global player but that also creates the temptation for corruption, which therefore requires that the resource find be balanced with the development of morally sound leaders, who would ensure that the profits from the resources benefit the entire country.

"This is where I come in. I have worked with presidents and governments across the world training leaders with integrity to run the affairs of nations and I have come to believe that leadership is key to the progress of any country or organization. If something goes wrong or right with the progress of a country or business it is always because of leadership," he said. Dr. Munroe said nothing happens, changes, improves, or is corrected without leadership and the state of the followers depends on the one leading them. So, if the leader is weak and incompetent that would reflect on the followers and eventually on the entire community, organization, or country.

He assured Ghanaians that during his meeting with business, political, community, and religious leaders, over the five days he is in Ghana, he would pass on very practical principle-based and purpose-driven leadership skills which have worked for him as the founder and owner of five successful global businesses, worked for his country, Bahamas, and for other countries and multinationals he mentors. "I would also be addressing the issue of national vision because without vision the country will go in circles, and I will also touch on youth development because the future of the country depends on the competencies of the youth," he said. Dr. Munroe and his ITWLA Team met with His Excellency Professor John Evans Atta Mills, the President of the Republic of Ghana for a private consultation and after speaking at a private worship service at the Presidential Palace of Sunday afternoon spent time in personal prayer with the head of state who did not hesitate to express his public faith in the Lord Jesus Christ and the role of Christ in his National governance. "I am deeply amazed, moved, and encouraged by His Excellency's openness with his Faith and his commitment to integrating the Kingdom of heaven's influence in his public duties. I hope many other world leaders would take the example of the President of Ghana and establish their public policies and national development programs on spiritual principles," said Dr. Munroe.[7]

Myles Munroe Visits Côte d'Ivoire

Ivory Coast, also known as Côte d'Ivoire, officially the Republic of Côte d'Ivoire, is a country of over 26 million people, located on the south coast of West Africa. Dr. Myles and Mama Ruth visited Ivory Coast in the early/mid-90s. There is little record of this trip except that they were invited to speak at a church conference. Mama Ruth told me of this trip, but she could not remember many details. Our goal was for Dr. Myles to reach every country in Africa and plans were already underway by the time of his departure for us to visit the northern African countries.

Myles Munroe Visits Eswatini (Swaziland)

MUNROE MAKES MAJOR IMPACT ON SWAZILAND AFRICAN KINGDOM

Bahamian Leadership Consultant and professional Coach, Dr. Myles Munroe was the special guest of His Majesty King Mswati III, King of Swaziland yesterday and was welcomed to the King's Palace by the Acting and Deputy Prime Minister Hon. Themba Masuku. Dr. Munroe arrived in Swaziland at the official invitation of the HRH King Mswati and the Government to facilitate a series of Leadership Training sessions. Over 300 members of the Government and administration of the Swaziland Kingdom attended the sessions including the Deputy Prime Minister, Hon. Themba Masuku, Minister of Tourism, Hon. Mduduzi D. Dlamini, Minister of Natural Resources and Energy, Hon. HRH Princess Tsandzile, Ministry of Economic Planning and Development, HRH Prince Hlangusemphi, and other members of the Cabinet. Dr. Munroe and his wife Ruth, along with their son and daughter, Charisa and Chairo, were honored guests of the King HRH Mswati III but were also the special guests of the Kingdom of Swaziland Ministry of Health. Dr. Munroe addressed the professional and Public Service staff and Administrators, medical professionals, support staff, and Permanent Secretaries about leadership. Minister of Health Hon. Benedict Xaba who served as principal host of the first national leadership event stated: "Dr. Munroe is exactly what our nation needed at this time and the response from all of our Cabinet members, Administrators and staff is evidence that he has impacted our community and nation in a real way. We all feel a new atmosphere of inspiration and a renewed spirit of hope in our air."

Dr. Munroe was welcomed into the royal courts of King Mswati III of Swaziland along with his wife Ruth, daughter Charisa, son Chairo and other members of his delegation including BFM's Television and Media Director, Agatha Christie, Director of Myles Munroe International South Africa's office, Mr. Charlie Masala, and his wife Xoli Masala, who flew with Dr. Munroe from Johannesburg, South Africa.

King Mswati III of the Kingdom of Swaziland was joined by members of his Government, Cabinet Ministers, his children, and members of the press welcoming Dr. Myles and Ruth Munroe and their family to the Royal Palace. The two leaders met for over one hour and discussed items ranging from the History of the Kingdom of Swaziland to the economic challenges facing the continent of Africa, and the future vision of Swaziland.

Dr. Myles and Mrs. Ruth Munroe and his entire delegation were then invited to join the HRH King Mswati III for one of the most historic cultural events of the Kingdom of Swaziland. His Majesty King Mswati III yesterday commissioned over 80 000 Imbali (maidens) to cut reeds at Mphisi Farm and Bhamsakhe during a colorful send-off at Ngabezweni Royal Residence yesterday afternoon.

Following long singing and ululating that was spiced up with glaringly unbridled excitement from the throngs of Imbali that are taking part in this year's Umhlanga Reed Dance, His Majesty finally emerged at around 4:30 p.m. to see off the maidens. The maidens started with a walk led by Inkhosatana Princess Sikhanyiso from Ludzidzini Royal Residence early in the morning to Ngabezweni where they were commissioned by the head of state to go and cut the reed.

Acting Prime Minister Themba Masuku said the maidens by once again coming in their numbers to be part of this year's Umhlanga just shows the unity that is holding this country together: "I wish the whole country a successful Umhlanga Ceremony because this was a unique cultural event that unites the nation."

Dr. Munroe and his son Chairo were invited by the King of Swaziland, His Majesty King Mswati to join him in the historic ceremony – Umhlanga and presented both with Royal Scepters to join in the celebration where over 100,000 jubilant young women and thousands of young men show a colorful display of song, dance, and shouts of unity unseen in any other nation. "I have never seen such organized joyful and dedicated unity among so many young people in one place," said Dr. Munroe.

The Umhlanga Ceremony sees 100,000 jubilant young women and thousands of young men show a colorful display of song, dance, and shouts of unity unseen in any other nation.

Dr. Munroe was then invited by His Majesty King Mswati III to return to the nation of Swaziland again in 2013 for four days of meetings and training programs for his government as well as a promise to call a national assembly of his citizens in the national stadium to be addressed by Dr. Munroe.

Dr. Munroe, his wife Ruth, and his delegation were then transported to a mass rally of over four thousand people with standing room only at the Jesus Calls Worship Center International hosted by Apostle Robert and HRH Princess Lindiwe Kasaro for a national Kingdom Event. The massive crowd rose to their feet with an explosion of shouts and whistles as Dr. Munroe was welcomed to the stage to address the excited citizens of the Kingdom of Swaziland about the Kingdom of God. "As a result of Dr. Munroe's message, tonight we are convinced that Swaziland is the Hope for the continent of Africa and that Dr. Munroe is the Hope for Swaziland," said Pastor Robert Kasaro.

Dr. Munroe left Swaziland today to return to Durban, South Africa, where he will address another Major Kingdom Conference Event hosted by Dr.'s. Basil and Anne Tryon of New Covenant Fellowship. Myles E. Munroe "Transforming Followers into Leaders and Leaders into Agents of Change."[8]

Dr. Myles and Mama Ruth's Love for the Holy Land of Israel

Dr. Myles Munroe's love and support for Israel dates to the early eighties when he was appointed Missions Director by Oral Roberts at the Oral Roberts University. Dr. Myles continued to organize tens of thousands of pilgrims to visit the Holy Land for three and half decades after that first visit. Dr. Myles loved Israel and he encouraged and influenced so many people to do the same, including me. I love the Holy Land and pray for the peace of Jerusalem as instructed by the constitution of my home country, the Bible.

I remember we were at the dinner table in May 2014 in Sandton, South Africa, with a group of business and politicians when one of them asked a question on Israel. The question was: "Dr. Myles, what is your stand on Israel with regards to human rights violations with regards to the situation with Palestine?" This question came about when Dr. Myles was indicating the importance of Israel in biblical history and prophecy but also as the land God chose originally as the model nation. Dr. Myles responded by saying that people should not confuse Israel and the Jews. Dr. Myles never confused the current politics of Israel and the Land of Promise. I have been privileged on several occasions to attend meetings where Dr. Myles addressed the Jewish meetings and I have heard him emphasize inclusion as there is now no Jew nor Gentile as we all have access through the blood of Jesus. Dr. Myles Munroe hated racism and apartheid as well as the oppression of humans by other humans.

I was fortunate to be invited and attended an event by the government of Israel honoring Dr. Myles Munroe in Jerusalem for his steadfast support to Israel. The event, which was held at the ninth annual 'Night to Honor our Christian Allies' on Jan. 29, 2015, honored Munroe for his "ongoing contribution to the Jewish state. According to Julie Stahl of CBN News, Christian Allies Caucus director Josh Reinstein thought that Munroe was courageous and had the "heart of a lion." "Myles Munroe was a true Israeli hero," Reinstein said. "He stood up unabashedly in a lot of countries where it's not popular to talk on behalf of Israel and say that he loves Israel; he loves the people of Israel; he loves the God of Israel; he loves the Bible of Israel."

Stahl reported that Tourism Minister Uzi Landau presented the Knesset Christian Allies Caucus and World Jewish Congress award to his son, Myles Munroe Jr., and daughter, Charisa. Reinstein added that Munroe "left such an impact on the government of Israel, the State of Israel, and its people." Charisa told CBN News that it was "an honor and privilege" for her parents to receive this award. "I'm prouder of my parents every day," Charisa said. "Every day, they show me how much they really loved the world and they really demonstrated that in everything they did around the world. It's definitely an honor." Munroe's son also elaborated on the legacy his father left to CBN News. "This shows the impact that both my parents had on, you know, the nation of Israel and on the world at large," Myles said. Myles added that "their ministry meant so much more than being in the Bahamas where they grew up. Their mandate was to go out into all the world," Myles said. "And, you know, I feel that's exactly what they did."

Gil Hoffman of the Jerusalem Post reported that the event took place at Jerusalem's Waldorf Astoria. He noted that Munroe, an evangelical pastor and motivational speaker based in the Bahamas, brought groups to the Jewish state twice a year.

Dr. Myles Munroe knew so much about the Holy Land to the point where he didn't need guides except that they came in handy to help him manage the two-week tours.

These tours were without a doubt the flagships of the Munroe calendar every year. I took pleasure in recruiting groups from South Africa to Israel yearly and I became Dr. Myles's assistant and was always at his side to carry his bag, camera, iPad, and Bible.

Dr. Myles' favorite holy sites in Jerusalem included, amongst others, the Garden of Gethsemane, Garden Tomb, Mount of Olives, and Dome of the Rock. In Galilee, his favorite sites included, amongst others, Mount Carmel where Elijah slew the prophets of Baal, boat ride in the sea of Galilee while he taught, Capernaum, the town of Jesus, Mount of Beatitudes (Matthew 5:3-11), Cana of Galilee (the wedding church), and the baptismal site of Yardenit located along the Jordan River in the Galilee region of northern Israel. It is there where an olive tree is planted in honor of Dr. Myles and Mama Ruth. Each time we visit the site we take pilgrims there to pay our respects as we remember Dr. Myles and Mama Ruth's love for the Holy Land.[9]

Dr. Myles Munroe with 3-Talk host, Noeleen
Maholwana-Sangqu, 2008

Celebrating Dr. Myles' 60th birthday in
Sandton, Johannesburg, South Africa, 2014

Dr Munroe with Papa Ezekiel Guti
in Zimbabwe, 2014

Dr. Munroe with the Malawi Visionary
Leadership

Visit to the DRC, 2012/2013

With the Olangis in the DRC, 2013

At the airport in Bujumbura, Burundi, 2014

Departing Burundi

Dr. Myles with Burundi President
Hon Pierre Nkurunziza

Dr. Myles Munroe arrives and greets the crowd in Gabon, 2014

Dr. Myles with Gabon host, Ps. Gaetan Piebi

Dr. Myles preaching with an intepreter in Gabon

Guests from Gabon celebrate Dr. Myles' 60th birthday in Johannesburg, 2014

Opening the door for Dr. Myles Munroe

Dr. Myles and Mama Ruth onstage in Uganda and attending a conference

Greeting President Yoweri Museveni of Uganda

Dr. Myles Munroe with First Lady Janet Museveni of Uganda

Dr. Myles Munroe with the President and First lady and Ugandan Parliment Staff

Media Interview in Uganda

Visit to Bali, Indonesia

Onstage in Bali, Indonesia

Dr. Myles Munroe with President John Atta Mills of Ghana, 2012

Dr. Myles with Timothy Kaberia of AFLEWO, Nairobi, Kenya in 2014

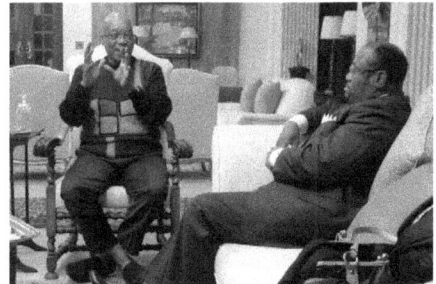

Dr. Myles with President Jacob Zuma, at his home in 2014, after the meeting concluded at 03:30

Visit to Jakarta, Indonesia

Visit to Eswatini (Swaziland)

Charlie with King Mswati III of Eswatini

Dr. Myles and Charlie with the Swazi
Deputy Prime Minister

Dr. Myles, Mama Ruth, Charisa, Charlie
and Guests with King Mswati III

Dr. Myles and King Mswati III at the
Mavuso Show Stadium

Dr. Myles and Mama Ruth
with King Mswati III

My Life and Times with Dr. Myles Munroe

The Munroes meeting with His Majesty the King Goodwill Zwelithini kaBhekuzulu in Durban, 2012

Dr. Myles Munroe with South African government and other political leaders

PART 4

LESSONS LEARNED FROM MYLES MUNROE

As a mentor and leadership coach to so many people around the world, including business and government leaders, Dr. Myles Munroe once said, "The passion of my life is to help as many people as possible, of every nation, race, creed, or social status, to discover their true leadership potential." Although his passing left a void that cannot be filled, his teachings remain a powerful and enduring legacy that continues to inspire us to fulfill our potential.

The quotes below are just some of Dr. Munroe's most inspirational and wisest sayings.

1. *The greatest tragedy in life is not death, but a life without a purpose.*

2. *I exist to transform followers into leaders.*
   My philosophy is: trapped in every follower is a leader.
   My belief is, if that person is placed in the right environment, the leader will manifest herself or himself.

3. *Every human heart cries and yearns for the same thing: a chance to fulfill his or her own dreams and desires.*

Even the poorest man has a dream.

4. Paradoxically, freedom requires the need to impose control on self, require more responsibility than slavery, and the decision to accept a destiny of freedom, recognizing the process and discipline that personal and political freedom require.

5. The greatness of a man is measured by the way he treats the little man. Compassion for the weak is a sign of greatness.

6. People generally fall into one of three groups: the few who make things happen, the many who watch things happen, and the overwhelming majority who have no notion of what happens. Every person is either a creator of fact or a creature of circumstance. He either puts color into his environment or, like a chameleon, takes color from his environment.

7. We are the sum of what we have learned from all who have taught us, both great and small.

8. The original purpose for a product determines its design, composition, capacity, and potential. Purpose may be defined as original intent or reason for creation.

9. We are smarter, not wiser, we live longer but not healthier, we have more but enjoy less, we go to the moon but not go home.

10. To exercise leadership, you must believe that you are inherently a leader.

11. *Leadership is not a right, but a privilege given by the followers.*

12. *There is nothing as powerful as an idea. Everything created began as an idea. Ideas created and still control the world. Pursue divine ideas.*

13. *Your existence is evidence that this generation needs something your life contains.*

14. *Purpose is when you know and understand what you were born to accomplish. Vision is when you see it in your mind and begin to imagine it.*

15. *The wealthiest places in the world are not gold mines, oil fields, diamond mines, or banks. The wealthiest place is the cemetery. There lies companies that were never started, masterpieces that were never painted. In the cemetery, there is buried the greatest treasure of untapped potential. There is a treasure within you that must come out. Don't go to the grave with your treasure still within you.*

16. *Circumstances and crises are God's tools to move you into your purpose and the maximizing of your potential.*

17. *The Creator caused to be inherent in each created entity – including the apex of his creation, mankind – everything it needs to fulfill its original purpose. The original purpose for mankind, defined and established by the Creator, was to "rule (have dominion) over all*

the earth." Since the word "dominion," in this case,

means to reign and rule, the Creator wired ALL human

beings with the capacity and natural ability to lead.

18. *Death can never kill an idea. Ideas are more powerful*

than death. Ideas outlive men and can never be

destroyed.

I celebrate Myles Munroe's contribution to the spiritual life of mankind with some of our favorite quotes on key topics:

On Leadership

You must become the answer to your own prayer for change in the world. The Creator caused to be inherent in each created entity – including the apex of his creation, mankind – everything it needs to fulfill its original purpose. The original purpose for mankind, defined and established by the Creator, was to "rule (have dominion) over all the earth." Since the word "dominion" in this case means to reign and rule, the Creator wired ALL human beings with the capacity and natural ability to lead.

> We are in a time where God is saying, "You do it! You fix it! You take action, because you are responsible for your society."

Leadership is not about control but service. It's not about power but empowerment. It's not about manipulation but inspiration. People generally fall into one of three groups: the few who make things happen, the many who watch things happen, and the overwhelming majority, who have no notion of what happens. Every person is either a creator of fact or a creature of circumstance. He either puts color into his environment or, like a chameleon, takes color from his environment. Solid character will reflect itself in consistent behavior, while poor character will seek to hide behind deceptive words and actions.

We are in a time where God is saying, *"You do it! You fix it! You take action, because you are responsible for your society."* God is telling us, "I want you to transform your society by taking leadership with Kingdom influence."

Jesus said, *"You go to the rooftops and shout out the truth!"* You are not responsible for people's responses, but you are responsible for the declaration of truth.

You can let things happen, or you can make things happen. We are called to act. Kingdom citizenship is a spiritual reality, but it is also a mentality. As believers, we already have the Spirit of God, but we need to learn the mind and the heart of God.

On Purpose

Your existence is evidence that this generation needs something that your life contains. Purpose is when you know and understand what you were born to accomplish.

Vision is when you see it in your mind and begin to imagine it. Circumstances and crises are God's tools to move you into your purpose and the maximizing of your potential. Don't be pushed by your problems; be led by your dreams.

Doing nothing is not an option; nations are imploding, social structures are collapsing…Whatever you allow, you can never criticize; whatever you avoid, you can never change. You must become the answer to your own prayer for change in the world. By refining your gift, you make room for it in the world. The more refined your gift, the more in demand you will be.

The wealthiest places in the world are not gold mines, oil fields, diamond mines, or banks. The wealthiest place is the cemetery. There lies companies that were never started, masterpieces that were never painted. In the cemetery, there is buried the greatest treasure of untapped potential. There is a treasure within you that must come out. Don't go to the grave with your treasure still within you.

On Potential

Be fruitful. God's command in Genesis 1:28 is most often understood as referring to procreation but filling the earth with people is only part of the meaning. God's purpose is that we bear abundant fruit and release the blessings of our gift and potential to the world.

Don't ever make the mistake of telling God that you have nothing to offer. That simply is not true. God does not create any junk.

You must decide if you are going to rob the world or bless it with the rich, valuable, potent, untapped resources locked away within you.

The more faithful we are with our stewardship the more resources God will entrust to us. That is a biblical principle. Don't be pushed by your problems; be led by your dreams.

On Success

Understand crisis and use it to solve a problem. Every business is a response to a problem. Initiate something; do not wait for things to be done. Identify and refine your talent, skill, idea, service, or knowledge to create wealth. Whatever makes you angry, you must solve it.

Poverty is not the lack of money, but the lack of ideas. God does not give cash, but ideas on how to create wealth. Be in control of your mind, thoughts, perception, and mentality to respond to change.

Be keen and take advantage of changes brought about by technology and globalization. Leave your legacy, but in the people that you train, not in products or buildings.

Every human being was born with a treasure. Your greatest secret to success lies in discovering your treasure.

On Dating and Relationships

Healthy relationships should always begin at the spiritual and intellectual levels – the levels of purpose, motivation, interests, dreams, and personality. The time you are most prepared for dating is when you don't need anyone to complete you, fulfill you, or instill in you a sense of worth or purpose. Being open to correction means making ourselves vulnerable, and many people are not willing to do that. Friendship is not a gift but is the result of hard work.

On Marriage

Marriage is the most important decision a person will make, next to his decision to follow Christ. A wedding is an event, but marriage is a life.

God did not create woman from man's head, that he should command her, nor from his feet, that she should be his slave, but rather from his side, that she should be near his heart.

The adversary's global attack on marriage is an attack on society itself, and ultimately an attack on God, the Creator, and Manufacturer of society and marriage. The adversary knows that if he can destroy marriage, he can destroy families; if he can destroy families, he can destroy society, and if he can destroy society, he can destroy humanity.

On Life

Life is not measured by duration but by donation. We are not to be so concerned about who approves or disapproves of us but remember that God's approval is what counts. Those whom God approves are approved indeed.

Proverbs 25:28 says, *"Like a city whose walls are broken down is a man who lacks self-control"* (NIV). In other words, if we do not control our own lives from the inside, somebody else will control them from the outside.

I'm washed, I'm forgiven, I'm whole, and I'm healed. I'm cleansed and I'm glory bound. I am only a sojourner on the earth. I am but a pilgrim on this planet, on my way to perfection, and I don't need anybody to tell me who I am, because I know who I am.

On Death

Dr. Myles believed and taught that if death finds you when you have poured out your life and have maximized your potential, you simply died; but if death finds you before you fulfill your purpose, you have been killed. Dr. Myles was not afraid of anything, including death. He often used to say, "The wealthiest spot on the planet is not the diamond mines of South Africa or the oil fields of Iran or Kuwait but the wealthiest spot on the planet is the graveyard. The greatest tragedy in life is not death but life without a purpose."

I honestly believe that Myles Munroe's work on the planet was completed. Thank God for technology; when you listen to him even today you can tell he was beyond his time and what we are learning, death cannot even take away. Many people have gotten to know him after death as they were exposed to his wisdom and teachings on the Kingdom of God. His death has propelled the Kingdom message. The way he died even made his messages go viral.

The Priority of Prayer

Besides the fact that Dr. Munroe wrote a book and taught on prayer, he prioritized prayer in his life. Both Dr. Myles and Mama Ruth fasted at least twice a year and they used to consecrate themselves and embarked into prayer and fasting for at least thirty days every January and they would dedicate time for prayer even during the year. He used to say that he got some revelations while communicating with God during a period of prayer and fasting. He led by example and from the front on this aspect. I genuinely believe it is one of the reasons why God used him so much.

His favorite line concerning prayer was: *"God has given mankind earthly license for heavenly interference. All that God is and all that God has may be received through prayer. Everything you need to fulfill your purpose on earth is available to you through prayer."* Dr. Munroe was always in prayer mode even though not religiously. Another of his favorite lines was, "Jesus is Lord!"

Total Dependency on the Commonwealth Economy of Heaven

Myles Munroe was dependent on the King's commonwealth. He believed in the King's supply to His Citizens. He believed in the Benevolence of our King, Jesus Christ. Someone gave him his first airplane. I saw Him walk in Kingdom supply and I learned to do the same. I depend only on the King. His supply is great and always on time. Most democracies base their economic systems on capitalism, which is a dangerous system. For capitalism to work there must be many poor people so that the labor costs less. This system capitalizes on the people. God's economic system is called commonwealth. It capitalizes on the King and not the people. God gave us rulership and not ownership. He has given mankind access to all the provisions in His commonwealth system.

On Publicists and Media Buying

Dr. Myles never required "spin doctors." He believed that his life should shine and so he didn't need publicists. He lived a unified life, so he considered his life an open book and a "city on the hill" that could not be hidden. He never compromised his Kingdom status. He had nothing to hide. Today we worry about our brands and how we look on our social media platforms. We are more concerned about how our profile photos look than the status of our lives and hearts. Myles Munroe's brand was his clean living, honesty, and exemplary life. Dr. Myles didn't believe in buying airtime to get his message around. His attitude was that if He was doing what God had told him to do and the message was effective, then the media had to follow him, and he did not need to chase them. I experienced this. Many media houses approached us wanting to air his content. Even today his content on YouTube and other media is highly sought after.

On Personal safety and Bodyguards

Dr. Myles Munroe had no bodyguards. He always quipped that his wife was his bodyguard. He had no fear. He always said that no one was looking for him to kill him and that he was a free man. He had no secrets as we had access to his iPad and phones, and he freely shared his passwords. He was indeed an open book. His home was accessible to everyone; he didn't live in a gated community. He always made himself available to

> Myles Munroe was dependent on the King's commonwealth. He believed in the King's supply to His Citizens. He believed in the Benevolence of our King, Jesus Christ.

people; he was the same man, whether at home, in big meetings, or at church.

He always invited his mentees to his space, including his home. Myles Munroe lived a simple life. I remember one evening when I was visiting him at his house, he invited Werner Gruner and me to accompany him on a hunt for Juju fruit (indigenous fruit in the Bahamas).

He had spotted the fruit tree while driving. I remember the three of us going to the tree and picking Juju fruit. It was an interesting visit and we all laughed. Dr. Myles was generally fearless. Even when visiting lion parks in Africa, which he liked doing on every trip, he would interact with the six-to-nine-month-old cubs, hold them and play with them. Those cubs were already the size of adult lions. He enjoyed the simplicity in life.

Be a People Person

I had the privilege of working with Dr. Myles Munroe closely for about two decades. He was an amazing individual. I remember him as some-one who was passionately against the oppression of human beings. He hated oppression; he hated the smell of it, he hated the sight of every-thing that had to do with the subjugation and dehumanizing of people. He was very much for human life. He was concerned about human life because he believed that God had hidden potential in everyone.

Whenever he was around people, Dr. Munroe was careful to give them his best attention. He wanted to nurture every gift that he recog-nized in them because you never knew who those people would become. One of his favorite sayings was, "Humans are never an interruption." He believed in every human being, and it did not matter whether they were Black, White, Indian, Colored, tall, short, educated, or illiterate, or what background they came from. He believed that humans are dynam-ic creatures and that we were created in God's image and likeness. There-fore, everybody is born with "divine deposits," which he called potential.

Dr. Myles Munroe held onto these ideals that were close to his heart right to the end of his life. From the time I first met him to the time he departed, he never changed his passion for loving people and paying attention to everybody. When you were with Myles Munroe, you would think you were the only person he loved. Because he loved everybody with a passion, he would make you feel special. He always wanted to make sure that you knew when you left his presence that you had been impacted and that he had given you his best. Sometimes that proved to be a challenge when he had finished a meeting and had to rush to another appointment. He was always prepared to give someone an autograph or engage in conversation with anyone who greeted him.

Myles Munroe impacted many lives. There are countless autographs of his all over the world. In one night, he could easily sign over a thousand books. People waited in long queues for him to autograph their books. People would come to him and share the vision and purpose for their lives, and he would listen to every story. He always said something to encourage them. He would pray with them and believe God for whatever they were believing God for. He gave his all to people everywhere. No matter how tired he was after a meeting, he would still give someone his attention.

Church or government leaders would often invite him for dinner, and we just knew it was not going to be a short visit. We would go there relaxed and unhurried, ready to enjoy the hospitality and conversation. We were prepared for all-nighters as these dinners could easily extend into the early hours. I think Myles Munroe was always at his best when he was around the dinner table. He shared many things around a meal when we are on the road. As I said, he was always at his best. He wouldn't keep quiet just because it was dinner time. People would listen, take notes, or record whatever he said. It was always interesting and informative. Most of the time he would be continuing with the subject that he had taught at an event unless people asked questions on other topics. It was as if he had left the meeting with the subject unfinished and wanted to continue and give you more sides to the topic. Dr. Munroe was always willing to answer questions because he said that it is the student who determines the lesson. "If you guys do not ask me questions you won't be able to learn," he would say. He encouraged us to ask questions all the time. He enjoyed being asked questions about what he had taught or be challenged on something he had said.

> Dr. Munroe taught me that there are things hidden in me that other people need and that I must be prepared to share them with the world. There are also things God has put in other people to bless me.

People who had a different understanding of a topic would often request deeper insights. His books reveal his vast knowledge of a variety of subjects. He could sit in a meeting and talk for hours about the contents of a book. Being familiar with his books, I could identify which publication he was quoting from, be it The Purpose and Power of Authority, The Most Important Person on Earth, or The Spirit of Leadership.

Be Adaptable

Dr. Munroe drew me in. There was nothing he would not make available for me. I still wear some of the vests and shirts he gave me. He was always prepared to lend me an item of clothing if I had forgotten to pack mine. Although he was shorter than me, he figured out that we wore a similar clothes size.

Once we were in the USA for an ITWLA meeting and I had no plans to travel to the Bahamas on that trip. However, Dr. Munroe suggested we fly to Nassau together and attend church the following day. He said I could always return to South Africa a day later. I told him that I hadn't packed enough clothes for an extended trip, but he said I shouldn't worry about it. When we arrived at his home, he gave me some pants to try on and assured me they would fit. I thought that there was no way those pants would fit me, yet when I tried them on, they fitted very well. Dr. Munroe smiled and said, "Let me tell you the secret. I wear my pants high, and you wear yours low. I knew that it would compensate for the height!" "Okay, Dr. Myles, I believe you!" I replied. I learned that a leader is not a leader who divorces himself from the people. A leader is not a leader because he appears to be in charge or "lords it" over people. You can be a leader without making anybody feel inferior.

Love One Another

I also learned the love for people. Before I met Myles Munroe, I was not too conscious of the value of humans. I just felt everybody could see things for themselves and sort themselves out. Dr. Munroe taught me that there are things hidden in me that other people need and that I must be prepared to share them with the world. There are also things God has put in other people which are there to bless me. He explained that that is why God did not create me alone; He created other people because there are things that he hid in others for me to be successful. You must know how to get along well with others because your blessing is locked up in other people. You must always treat everybody as important because you don't know who they were born to be. He used to say that we should handle people with care because they might be your next boss! Even in a confused society where roles are switched, we should handle everybody as important because of who they are in God. We were created in God's image so each time you mistreat someone you must take it that you are mistreating God.

Keep Things in Perspective

He also taught me to be flexible. It should not feel strange to go to strange places. We should feel as comfortable visiting poor people at their homes as we do rich people. A particular environment should not dictate my response. My response should always be consistent. We could go to any place and use any car. There are many instances where Dr. Munroe would get into a cheap car that was not even meant for him and say, "Yes, it's fine, let's use this."

I learned simplicity even though Myles Munroe was not a poor man. He didn't take the things of this world too seriously. He didn't feel that he needed to have a glass house or twenty Rolls Royces. He lived a very practical life and used a practical car. He had a Jaguar that he drove for eleven years or more. He drove it to the point where the roof lining was coming loose. He would drive this car and never even worry about it. He would get into the car and say, "Charlie, let's go change the world!"

He used to drive fast. He would play his own tapes and CDs in the car, which I found a little strange but got used to it. I always took what Myles Munroe did very seriously because I knew there was a reason for everything he did. Even if it did not make any sense to me, I always knew he had a reason for whatever he was doing. Even if he was driving an aging car, I knew it was deliberate. He always said that what we drive or wear does not define us. For example, if a king wears a plastic shoe it is not plastic, it is royal plastic. He said I am the one who gives value to the things I use. Whenever we drove somewhere together, he would listen to the message on a CD and then talk about its meaning. He would also talk about many different things in life. He taught me that life is not much about the accumulation of things. There is more to life. I must understand that God gives me things not only because he has me in mind but because He has others in mind too.

Be a Generous Servant Leader

Myles Munroe believed in sharing. It didn't matter what car he arrived in. It was neither here nor there. That was a big lesson. When I first visited his house, I realized that it was a modest house. He also taught me that men can cook. He said that it was alright for a man to cook. He was a good cook and could fix delicious ribs.

He was particularly good at ribs. He was happy to share kitchen duties with his wife too. Each time we got back to his house after church, you knew that Dr. Myles Munroe was going to change his clothes and head for the kitchen. Whenever I stayed at their house, he would wake me up early and fix me breakfast. He would knock on my door and say, "Hey, get up! It's not South Africa. Come, let's have breakfast!"

Always Be in Control

He always had energy. He taught me that you must always be in control of your surroundings. You might not control what happens to you, but you must control how you respond to it. He taught me that you can always be in charge of your surroundings.

Myles Munroe enjoyed life. He always laughed at things and enjoyed jokes. I often made him laugh because when I was young, people would gather around, and I used to crack jokes. When I was with him privately, I would operate in that gift. My jokes were a little more advanced because they were always relevant and fresh and usually about something we had heard when visiting a place. We would generally ignore a humorous incident at the time and then bring it up later when we were alone. I would imitate someone who had funny mannerisms or acted peculiarly, and we would laugh about it. Once when we were in eSwatini, I went outside to fetch something from the car. On my way back, the queens happened to be walking somewhere at the same time.

Sihle, the King's aide, shouted, "Hey Charlie, don't look at the Queens!" Dr. Munroe always found that funny and I would bring it up whenever we felt tired or in need of some light relief. He would say, "Charlie, don't look at the Queens!" Sometimes I would imitate his teaching and the tone of voice he used in his earlier messages. He would laugh at that. I used to make him feel at ease when we were on the road.

Each time I called Dr. Myles to wake him up in the morning while we were abroad, he would always answer like someone who was up, prepared, and just waiting for my call. The energy in this servant-leader was just amazing.

Value Your Family

Myles Munroe also taught me to value family. He was a big advocate of family and marriage. He would even tell the church that if they were sick and his wife was looking for him then there would be a funeral because he was going home to his wife and family! He loved his wife and kids. The first person that Dr. Myles Munroe would introduce was his wife. This was standard practice. It didn't matter if they were meeting Heads of State, he would always introduce his wife first. If she were still walking into a place, he would wait until she arrived and then introduce her. He always made sure that his wife was taken care of. If he couldn't see her, he would ask where she was and didn't want to move until he knew her whereabouts. They had an exceptionally great working and marriage relationship. I learned to honor my wife in public from Dr. Myles Munroe because he did that all the time without fail.

I value my family today because of that lesson I learned from him. Whenever I am speaking in a place, I want to make sure that my wife is the first person I take with me like Dr. Munroe used to do. He had a picture of his family at the beginning of his PowerPoint presentations. It was one of the first things he would mention when he went onstage. I do the same thing wherever I speak.

Dr. Myles Munroe would also have loved to see his legacy of marriage continue. He believed that a strong marriage yields strong leaders. I think he would have loved to see marriage become more and more a culture since the real concept of marriage is being eroded. Given this dedication to encouraging godly marriage, he would also have loved to educate people that homosexuality is not God s will. He wanted to prove to the world that that system is not God's design and is not sustainable. He would have loved to continue with that message.

Live by Faith

Dr. Myles Munroe taught me faith. He was unshakable. You could never shake his faith. Even if something bad occurred somewhere, he was always steady in his faith.

I learned that even when there is no provision, I know that the provision will come. We cannot allow ourselves to be shaken when there is a shortage of money and we are behind on the mortgage. I have learned not to just take things at face value but to see beyond that to what could be. Sometimes the budget on a trip would not be working and Dr. Munroe would say, "Don't worry about it. Jesus is Lord!" He liked to say that Jesus is Lord. You could recognize when he was deep in thought, and he would just turn around and say "Jesus is Lord!" He would also say it whenever he had to deal with something he knew was beyond his ability to handle it.

In his teachings on the Kingdom Concept of Lordship, Dr. Munroe revealed that Jesus is Lord because he is the Owner. The word "lord" comes from the word adorn. When we acknowledge His lordship, we acknowledge His ownership. If Dr. Munroe needed something, he would say, "Well, Jesus is Lord, Jesus is the owner. I need not worry about these things because Jesus is the owner." You would never see any sign of desperation on his face; he would never despair at all. He would just be steady and say, "Don't worry, my son, the Lord will provide. Life goes on."

See the Best in Others

I also learned from Myles Munroe that we must give people second chances in life. People whom you trusted to do certain things will disappoint you, but never lose faith in them. I learned that you could strike that balance. Dr. Munroe was prepared to do anything; he would not ask you to do something he wouldn't do. If you promised to do something for him and he saw it had not been done, he would finish the task himself. He taught me that you should give people chances in life. There must

> I learned that even when there is no provision, I know the provision will come. We cannot allow ourselves to be shaken when there is a shortage of money and we are behind on the mortgage.

always be a second or third chance for someone; even if they disappoint you again, you must still give them another chance. I learned that from him and partly learned it from my dad. This is also an aspect of hard work—being prepared to complete a task for someone who could not complete it themselves for whatever reason.

Always be Prepared to Work

Myles Munroe was a hard worker; He was always working. He would sometimes be sweating after leaving a meeting and the Holy Spirit's presence had been heavy there. When we boarded the plane after that, he would say, "Jesus is Lord," and then rest awhile. But it wouldn't be long before he asked, "Where is my computer?" He would get to work right away. He worked on his PowerPoint presentations or books.

He would prepare his messages between meetings. Dr. Myles Munroe taught me to be prepared for anything. This has helped me because I occasionally get into situations where I'm asked to do something without warning. For example, a deacon forgets to inform me that I had to receive the offering. They would only tell me that morning when I arrived at church. I have learned to always stay ready to deliver a particular service or even be forced to speak in public without warning. Dr. Munroe often did that to me.

Be Flexible

We must always be flexible when dealing with different levels of people. We must be adaptable. Dr. Munroe could address diverse audiences on the same day—children, public servants, company employees, or churchgoers—with the same quality but different levels of delivery. You use different language when speaking to a politician than when you are speaking to the clergy. Dr. Munroe taught me how to engage with people in a way that they would take you seriously and you would still get something out of it.

Myles Munroe was always in the driver's seat. It didn't matter whether he was meeting heads of state, kings, and top sports or business personalities, he was always the one asking questions. With Heads of State, he would use a "questioning style" of communication, and where there were gaps in knowledge, he would close them. He would ask questions and let them talk. Then he would talk about the economy of that country, issues of social justice, labor, etc. He would always address government leaders on relevant issues.

Once people engaged Myles Munroe in conversation, it would be difficult for them to leave. I remember many places where they would say that he only had thirty minutes because the president, king, or prime minister, had to attend another engagement. They would end up postponing their next meeting. He once had an interview on eTV, a major news channel in South Africa. They rarely exceeded the allocated time on the morning shows. You would wake up at 04:00 or 04:30 and prepare yourself to be on air for only four minutes. That is a long time on prime-time national television. On that occasion, Dr. Myles Munroe ended up doing the whole morning show. We were there for forty-five minutes. You couldn't let him go when he was speaking; you just wanted to draw more out of him. He had a style that I am hoping to perfect one day. It didn't matter to Myles Munroe whether the interviewer was good or bad. If he had a good interviewer then he would flow with them but with a "bad" interviewer, he would take over and lead the conversation.

Understand the Kingdom

I learned so many lessons from Myles Munroe, yet there are many more. He taught that prayer is communication with God. Prayer is not just a religious act where you must wear a shawl. Dr. Myles would pray many times in a day without formally announcing that he was praying. He would just speak softly… thank you, Lord… Jesus is Lord… and you would realize he was praying. He could do that without acting "religious" or making others feel prayerless. He was excellent at that.

One of the main things he taught me, which I hadn't learned as a regular churchgoer, was the Kingdom of God. I learned that the Kingdom of

God is not a religion. There is a difference between the Kingdom of God and Christianity. It is linked to God's purpose for our lives. God sent us from heaven to earth to represent Him because He is a spirit and spirits cannot operate in the physical realm in that form. So, God sent us. We are also spirits because we are made in His image and likeness. God put us in an "earth suit" to invade earth on His behalf. A Kingdom citizen is not a religious person. You are a representative of heaven showing His culture and demonstrating what heaven is like on earth.

I have learned that there is a difference between the Kingdom of God and the Kingdom of heaven. The Kingdom of heaven is a place, but the Kingdom of God is a system. For example, the well-known Bible verse in John 3:16 says, *"For God so loved the world that He gave His only begotten Son, that whoever believes in Him should not perish but have everlasting life"* (NKJV, emphasis added). God loves people and everything else He created. The word "world" in the above verse comes from terra, which means earth. It includes trees, mountains, rivers, creatures, and the universe with its countless planets and stars. God loves the systems of heaven operating in the world. The world's systems can create hell for you on the earth, but heaven's systems can create an environment where people live together in harmony.

Dr. Myles Munroe was knowledgeable on most topics. I learned by observing him that you can be knowledgeable and still be a person of God. Dr. Munroe could participate intelligently in any discussion. Whether you were talking about airplanes, war, hunger, colonization, politics, or anything else, he had something to say about it. Kingdom principles offer solutions to the world's problems. I think he was one of the few people who had gotten a revelation to that extent. I know that many pastors don't accept the Kingdom message the way he taught it because you need to have that revelation. Many believers say that Christianity is a relationship, but Dr. Myles Munroe taught that Christianity is a religion. We are supposed to be like Jesus and Jesus was not a Christian. It is not about having a title. God wants His followers to be Christ-like and not just act Christlike.

People in Antioch originally used the term "Christian" in a derogatory way to mock followers of Christ. We are fighting for a title that God never called us because He never called us Christians. Myles Munroe helped me to understand the *difference* between Christianity and the Kingdom of God. He defined the Kingdom of God as "God's influence over a territory, impacting it with His will, intentions, and culture."

The word "kingdom" comes from two words: king and domain. When the Kingdom of God influences a territory, it becomes the king's domain. God wants His Kingdom to influence the whole earth. I have heard preachers say that the Kingdom of God is about doing things right. What does that mean? It sounds good but how do I teach it to people so that they understand what the Kingdom of God is. We need to learn about the Kingdom so we can live by its principles. Then the Gospel of the Kingdom can spread to the ends of the earth as God intended.

See the Lighter Side of Life

I learned from Dr. Munroe that leaders must be able to laugh at life. Sometimes he got into a situation where he would just laugh. If he ever met someone who didn't know who he was, he would never say, "Don't you know who I am? I'm Myles Munroe. I write books!" In those situations, he would always humble himself.

Sometimes he went to places where someone would say something untoward, and Dr. Munroe would just laugh it off. Where most people would end up arguing, he would be ready with that laugh of his. He said that when you don't fight back you disarm your enemy. I found that interesting because most of us want to make sure we can prove a point. He always said that he didn't want to win an argument and lose a friend.

Serve God Not Money

I learned that money is not everything. That is an important lesson. Occasionally, Dr. Munroe would speak at an event and the person hosting us had to pay a certain amount. When Dr. Munroe realized that the host had no intention to pay him or was unable to, he would always walk away and not get into an argument about money. It goes back to where he said you may win an argument but lose a friend. In cases like that, you should rather walk away and keep the friendship. Myles Munroe was too busy to hold grudges. Sometimes people who owed us money would try to invite us again and Dr. Munroe would be prepared to go. As an Administrator, I would remember who had done us in but Dr. Munroe would say, "Nobody can steal from me. You can't steal anything from me. I am a Kingdom man. I am a real man of God. They can't steal from me. When you steal from me you steal from God."

I remember a situation where someone we worked with went behind our backs and sued a client that we had decided not to sue. He went to court and won the case. He pocketed the money to the tune of 1.8 million Rand from a two-million-rand contract. When we learned of this, we approached the guy and asked him about it. He acted indifferently, but Dr. Munroe just said that when you steal from him you were stealing from God. He left such situations in God's hands. I, on the other hand, believed we should still do something about it. I desperately wanted to send him a letter and demand our money. Myles Junior and I still felt we should sue.

Knowing that someone is enjoying your 1.8 million when you can't meet your financial obligations at the office is not a good thought to have. Dr. Myles Munroe was a kind man who didn't like disputes. He loved to promote unity because where there is unity there are blessings. He taught me that money is not everything.

True value is found in people. Dr. Munroe taught me that you are valuable even when people around you don't think so. He taught me to always be confident because my value is not based on their opinion of me. Sometimes people will take you for granted, so don't take it personally. If you know who you are in Christ, you will not let the ignorance of others affect you. When people nailed Jesus to the cross, He prayed that the Father would forgive them because they were unaware of what they were doing. Those who are spiritually mature are the ones who forgive. If people knew better, they would not do the things they were doing. Once you discover that the person is doing what they are doing because of ignorance you should forgive them right away he says.

Respect Authority

I learned to never take authority that I had not been given. Dr. Myles

Munroe would always respect and submit to his hosts. If we arrived at a church, even of one hundred people, he would say that the pastor was the authority in that house and so we would submit to him. He always made that clear to our host. Attendees could not sway him either. Sometimes we would go to a meeting where the host loved Dr. Munroe and his message and wanted the people to receive the message. The host was not the wealthiest or most influential person in town and people richer than he would attend the event. Dr. Munroe would never allow those so-called well-to-do people to overshadow his host or disrespect the host. He always respected his host. He understood authority.

> Dr. Myles would always respect and submit to his hosts. If we arrived at a church, even of one hundred people, he would say that the pastor was the authority in the house and so we would submit to him.

Another example is that Dr. Myles Munroe put me in charge of the Africa office. He said that everything regarding the Africa region had to come through me. Dr. Munroe told me he had placed me as the authority there and not even He could defy and disrespect that authority. If someone was looking to host or meet Dr. Munroe, they had to go through me, regardless of what they thought of me or if they had a "higher station" in life. Dr. Munroe was prepared to tell them as much. He would also never go with someone who was only attending a meeting. He only went where his authority took him. I learned a lot from that. Even when I travel to minister at churches and other places, I sometimes meet people who think they are cleverer than my host and claim that they could have done a better job of hosting me. In such cases, I always call them to order.

Dr. Munroe said that you shouldn't be afraid to rebuke what is wrong, there and then. Do not take it personally and just move on. He was once a guest on a live television show that a prominent media personality hosted at the South African Broadcasting Corporation (SABC). Something happened that made the host of the show cuss (swear). When she remembered that Dr. Munroe was sitting close to her, she apologized profusely, saying, "Sorry, sorry, excuse me, Dr. Myles!" He said to her, "Don't worry about it. It was in your heart." He was a very open-spirited person; he didn't keep secrets and would just say it as he saw it.

We once went to visit former South African president, Jacob Zuma. As I recall it was April 2014. We got there about 11p.m. and the president arrived after us. He was very tired from a whole day of canvassing ahead of the general elections in May that year. His staff took care of him as he first wanted to freshen up. We waited for him to come through to the room where we were seated. During that meeting, Dr. Munroe began talking about different pertinent and controversial issues which were trending in the public domain at the time. He was not shy to ask tough questions. These included Zuma's rape case (the Johannesburg High Court dismissed those charges in May 2006), and Nkandla (In March 2016, the Constitutional Court ordered Zuma to pay back a portion of State funds used to build his homestead in Nkandla, Kwazulu-Natal). Dr. Munroe asked him about everything. There is nothing he didn't ask.

It was a closed meeting, and the media were not present. It was a very revealing meeting. I saw a side to Jacob Zuma that many people may be unaware of. I sat there thinking that Dr. Munroe had stepped over the line, yet Zuma answered every question in detail. We gained a new respect for President Zuma and realized then that he was a real politician. Dr. Munroe was not afraid to be vulnerable because when you ask questions like those you run the risk of your host refusing to answer or humiliating you by saying, "I don't think you are the person to ask me these questions." Dr. Munroe displayed boldness in asking about sensitive issues, while President Zuma showed he was accommodating and open-minded. This is also remarkable because we started our meeting late at night and only left there around 3a.m. President Zuma still had to wake up early that Monday morning to attend a National Executive Committee meeting at Luthuli House, the ANC headquarters in Johannesburg. The former president must have been impressed with Dr. Munroe because he invited him to attend his inauguration after that visit!

Be Yourself

You must not be afraid to be who God called you to be. Always be prepared to show people who you are. Myles Munroe was not shy to come across as confident. He once asked me if I knew why he put his face on most of his books. I didn't, so he explained that he wanted people to know that Myles Munroe was black. He wanted to restore the dignity of the Black man. He was not afraid to say that he was very much aware of who he was and how powerful in the world he was. However, he didn't use that power to subjugate, hurt, or look down upon anyone, or make other people feel inadequate. Sometimes we would leave a place and I would say, "Dr. Myles, the way you tackled that interview was powerful."

He would just smile and say, "You don't know me, Charlie. I'm a dangerous man." He would repeat it over and over. He would act the same way whenever we met some of these so-called "big" ministers. They never intimidated him. And he would say things that blew their minds. It didn't matter who he was meeting, Dr. Munroe could hold his ground and stick to his guns. He was never intimidated by anyone.

He was not afraid to be different because many popular preachers do not understand the Kingdom message. They understand Christianity, religion, and biblical history but not necessarily the Kingdom of God. That is why most of them run away from political spaces because they think it is out of bounds. They don't realize that politics is important because politics is where you reclaim the environment that the church has lost.

Myles Munroe was not afraid to call "kings" to order. He told some of them that until they repented, he would not speak for them anymore. By the time he passed, there were places where he was not speaking anymore. I will protect the names of those people. He was no longer preaching for some people that we respected very much; he was disappointed over them. He was disappointed in some who were using the Bible to hide the fact that they were gay.

Dr. Myles Munroe discusses authority in his book, The Purpose and Power of Authority. He told those popular personalities that they must submit themselves to an authority figure. He said they must find a spiritual father. They were out of order because nobody could tell them anything. No matter how important you become, you must always be under an authority figure who is not afraid of you and who doesn't want anything from you. Anyone who is a spiritual father can speak objectively into your life. Many that they call "sons" are not sons at all but supporters whom they cannot tell anything because they are afraid to lose their monthly contributions. He says that when he is the father figure, he is not looking for anything from a son because he must be able to rebuke you.

Learn to Lead

Dr. Myles Munroe was always learning and was well-read. He read at least four books a month, plus magazines and other sources of knowledge. He always asked questions. Whether visiting a game park, cultural center, or museum, he would always engage with the rangers and guides. As a leader, you must know that you are leading leaders as well. You are the leader of leaders. Myles Munroe was always confident. Even among other leaders that he was serving with he always came across as confident. He was always very aware that he was leading people who were leaders themselves. He could balance committee dynamics very well.

Sometimes he would inform the committee that there was an issue but that they could work around it. He would always have a solution, but he would give you space to function and contribute. He always knew what he wanted to do about something. He would make his intended direction clear and ask others how they could support him to do that. He made a way for others to offer supportive ideas without attempting to counteract his plans.

Dr. Myles Munroe was a people person. I learned from him that when you laugh or even dance with others it doesn't make you inferior to them. I also learned from him that knowledge makes you feel confident. If you are learned about a subject, you will be confident and have more answers. No one could corner him. I never met anyone who could corner him where he was forced to say, "I'm not sure. I'll have to go and read more about it." He always came across as convincing and clear on what he believed about something. He always came across as an authority on any subject.

He was not afraid to have a difference of opinion, no matter whether he was addressing Bahamian government leaders or fellow church leaders who were out of order. This is all part of learning to lead.

Develop Godly Character

Myles Munroe felt that for the church to be effective there is only one message that the church can preach and that is the Kingdom of God transforming societies.

According to Dr. Munroe, real pastors who understand the Kingdom of God should be able to address the president of the country. You should be able to speak to ministers without a problem, but you malfunction when you don't understand that principle. You must understand that, as a Kingdom citizen, you have power and are operating in an office that is entirely different and more authoritative than any other. You must know what you stand for. You cannot confidently invite someone to preach at your church when you are unsure of what they stand for or what error they might preach.

Dr. Munroe felt that leaders are not being effective because they are not administering the right solution to a hurting world and the confused leaders of our nations. Another reason the church has lost effectiveness is the lack of character in leadership. He felt very strongly that Kingdom leaders are supposed to be people of character who cannot easily be swayed or bribed. Church effectiveness is lost where grace is abused. Grace is "the state of kindness and favor toward someone, often with a focus on a benefit given to the object" (Strong's Greek 5485). In the church, we preach righteousness, but some churchgoers and pastors don't want to hear it; they only want to hear about "grace." However, you cannot separate the two.

Righteousness is a legal term that means "right standing" with God. We abuse God's grace when we know the price that Christ paid to set us free, yet we continue to live sinful lives. What should a judge do after he gives you a lesser sentence and you commit the same crime again? The government rightfully punishes you when you commit a crime because you are not in right standing with it. God's grace means He does not treat us as our sins deserve (Psalm 103:10-12). Our only reasonable response is to turn away from sin and live a righteous life. Only then is our church positioned to regain its effectiveness.

He always said he only had one wife and two children on the planet. He was who he was and had no skeletons in the closet. His powerful book, The Power of Character in Leadership, contains the names of many contemporary leaders who had moral failures. He was not shy to talk about leadership failures. Some of the names in the book will be familiar to you. He speaks about a "crisis of character" in contemporary leadership. He identified the missing element in leadership as "the moral force." He discusses many moral failures in politics, including in the

Obama administration, the impeachment of Bill Clinton, and Anthony Weiner, the New York congressman who was jailed after sending explicit text messages and photographs to several women. Weiner even ran for Mayor of New York City after resigning from Congress in the wake of his sexting scandal!

The Iran-Contra affair occurred during US president Ronald Reagan's second term. The scandal erupted in 1986 after senior administration officials sold arms to Iran to secure the release of American hostages in Lebanon. In 1974, in the wake of the Watergate scandal, Richard Nixon became the first US President to resign.

In 2012, the High Court in Brazil sentenced José Neto, former president of the governing Worker's Party, to jail for his role in a vote-buying scheme. The President of Kenya, Uhuru Kenyatta, and his deputy, William Ruto, faced charges for crimes against humanity by the International Criminal Court for post-election violence in 2013. The Yugoslavia War Tribunal of the United Nations convicted six Bosnian political and military leaders for persecuting and murdering Muslims during the Bosnian war.

Leadership moral failures are not limited to politics. Prominent investment bankers, JP Morgan and Chase, faced fines totaling about $1 billion for market manipulation and risk management practices.

> Church effectiveness is lost where grace is abused. Grace is "the state of kindness and favor toward someone, often with a focus on a benefit given to the object"

Sexual abuse allegations have been lodged against Catholic priests in nations around the world. Cover-ups and inaction by church officials have fueled outrage. Atlanta megachurch bishop, Eddie Long, was accused of sexually abusing four teenagers. These were people that he spoke for. Bishop Long maintained his innocence but reportedly settled out of court with the plaintiffs.

In a separate case, ten church members filed a civil lawsuit against Long whom they allege used his influence to get them to invest in a pyramid scheme. Once prominent televangelist, Jimmy Swaggart, became immersed in a scandal involving a prostitute. Televangelist, Jim Bakker, was also caught up in a scandal due to an adulterous relationship with a former church secretary. Bakker was jailed for fraud and conspiracy related to his ministry's fundraising. Ted Haggard resigned as pastor of his church in Colorado and as President of the National Association of Evangelicals after a homosexual affair with a male prostitute as well as illegal drug use. Dr. Munroe was able to call out sin in society because he lived a clean life.

Disciple the Nations

When we talk about the Church, it must include the broader perspective. Dr. Myles Munroe made me believe that the world was my playground. He helped me believe that I could do something that would touch the four corners of the globe. He made me realize that God placed things in me which the world would only know when I become who I was born to become. I was born to be a gift to the world, and I mus become that gift. He pointed out that the Church is not becoming the godly agency that

God sent it to become. The Church is too busy lighting candles, burning incense, and following rituals instead of following God's lead of taking charge of the world.

Despite being the Ecclesia (called-out ones), the church has become more of a problem than a solution. Dr. Munroe believed there should be no difference between Church and State. The world belongs to God. Therefore, God's influence should be found in every place and not just one place called the church. The church is not a building we go to. We are the church. We are God's temple. A change in mindset is needed. The world systems are happy to have the church not knowing its rightful place and sidelining it when it is supposed to be at the heartbeat of the nations. God called the nations to become the ambassadors of the Kingdom of Heaven on the earth. God put nations in place to disciple believers back to God.

Dr. Munroe taught me that the church is a powerful weapon. The problem is that the church has become ineffective in the hands of religious leaders who themselves have become irrelevant because they are pushing church programs and not the Kingdom agenda. We are to make disciples of nations not just disciples of people.

National salvation is vital in countries like South Africa. People must fight for the salvation of their nation. Nations should not be passing laws that are against the Kingdom agenda.

To disciple the nations, we cannot just speak church language to church people but must speak the Kingdom agenda with people in politics. The church must be involved in politics to fulfill that Kingdom mandate. Myles Munroe always said that he did not believe in Christian government, but Holy Spirit-filled believers should be involved in government activities. We must have true believers in government if we are to eradicate corruption. The Kingdom of God must influence government and it does not have to be a Christian government.

Our agenda for South Africa and the rest of Africa was clear. We were not focused on having big crusades. Dr. Munroe wanted to disciple nations by influencing national leadership. He said, "If I change the leaders, I change the nation." If you change a leader's thinking it has a knock-on effect. Dr. Munroe said it was especially important to influence changes in legislation. He happened to be in South Africa when an American televangelist was here and commented that he would rather talk to thirty political leaders than to ten thousand others. "I don't know how we missed it because the Bible doesn't say make disciples of these people; it says make disciples of nations."

To disciple the leaders of nations, it is crucial to not be intimated by anyone or see yourself as inferior. An example of this is our meeting with Pierre Nkurunziza, the longest-serving president of Burundi. We almost did not attend that meeting because the hosts were reluctant to allow Dr. Munroe's entourage to accompany him.

However, the Burundian government allowed us entry after we informed them that Dr. Myles Munroe would be unable to accept their invitation if his team could not go with him. A similar situation occurred in Tanzania. Dr. Munroe made it clear that if we were not going then he was not going either! Dr. Munroe always insisted that we be there. He wanted his team to meet high-profile leaders together with him so we could learn to interact with them respectfully but with boldness.

Get Wisdom and Understanding

Myles Munroe believed that love is not enough. Ask divorcees if they still loved each other and the answer is usually, "Yes, but we can't live together." Dr. Munroe liked to quote Proverbs 24:3, "Through wisdom a house is built, And by understanding it is established" (NKJV). He always encouraged people to get wisdom and understanding so they could know what they were doing. When you get knowledge, it can bring understanding. Once you have gained understanding, the thing you desire can be yours. When you apply what you know, you are acting with wisdom. Wisdom is the correct application of knowledge (see James 2:20).

Freedom from Oppression

Dr. Myles Munroe was passionate about several things. One which stands out was his passion for people to experience real freedom, especially those with Third World backgrounds. He wanted them to be free from the colonial oppression they had suffered for so many years. This was not just freedom from spiritual oppression, although that was one of Munroe's passions; he wanted people to have economic freedom. And it is important to realize that it is not just colonialists who oppress people, but self-serving leaders. In South Africa, political role-players like to use slogans like "Economic Freedom in our Lifetime" and "Radical Economic Transformation," but the question is who benefits most from these initiatives?

I think Myles Munroe discovered his passion for economic freedom at a young age, having grown up in the Bahamas when it was still a British colony. As discussed earlier in this book, South Africa and the Bahamas share a similar history. Nelson Mandela and former Bahamian Prime Minister, Sir Lynden Pindling, attended university together in London. Pindling led the Bahamas to majority rule on 10 January 1967 and independence on 10 July 1973. He served as its first black Premier from 1967 to 1969 and Prime Minister from 1969 to 1992. Myles Munroe became a good friend of Pindling, who officially recognized him when Munroe was leading a youth band called "Visionary." One of Munroe's most popular tracks, Brand New World, spoke of how people are trying everything to change their lives, but the answer is only found in Christ.

> Dr. Myles Munroe discovered that when the Bible talks about freedom, it is not just referring to freedom of religion but freedom of living where people can become who they were born to be.

Munroe used to speak about his anger at growing up in a colonized environment. When he became a believer in Jesus Christ, he realized there was a stark contrast between God's Word and their way of life. His father was a lay pastor, and they would talk about how God owns "the cattle on a thousand hills," yet they didn't have any beef. They had no access to many benefits and could not enjoy the meat of those cattle on the hills. The system advantaged one people group in the Bahamas as it did in South Africa. It allowed those people to get ahead in life while restricting others.

Seeing that oppression gave Myles Munroe a burden to deliver people around the world who were in similar situations, as we were in South Africa. His experience in the Bahamas gave him a clear picture of how such systems were operating around the world. His main passion was to free the people. He knew it was not only political freedom; there was another level of freedom which was mental freedom. He realized people were not free because their mind, and not people, was keeping them in bondage. This is because we came from a system that conditioned us to think in a particular way. Munroe also realized that people would need a higher level of help to get free of that conditioning. He was able to tap into that other world which is the spiritual world.

Dr. Myles Munroe discovered that when the Bible talks about freedom, it is not just referring to freedom of religion but freedom of living where people can become who they were born to be. I remember him telling me about the story of Martin Luther King Jr. and Malcolm X. We were talking about freedom, and he said, "Charlie, do you know why Martin Luther King Jr. was more popular than Malcolm X?" I didn't, so he continued, "Besides the fact that Malcolm X was Muslim, and many people have an allergy towards Islam, the main thing was that Martin Luther King Jr. fought for civil rights. That is why they call that movement the 'civil rights movement.' When you fight for civil rights, you are fighting for inclusion. You want to be included in civic activities. Civil rights are the right to be civilized."

He said that even though what Martin Luther King Jr. fought for was important, what excited Munroe most about Malcolm X was that he fought for the right to be human—the human right. He said the right to be human is the right that we all want, which is the right to become everything we were born to be, to give our gifts to the world, and to deliver what we were born to deliver to the world. He described that as the highest form of struggle. When you fight for people to be included in the civic happenings in your country, you also fight for them to be recognized as human. All people are human, and not just whites. People must be allowed to become who they were born to be and to live out the gifts that God has endowed them with.

Have a Unified Vision With a Goal to Impact Your Nation

Another of Myles Munroe's main passions was church. I think he loved the church. And he was particularly passionate about the Kingdom message. He realized that very few ministers had received the revelation of the Kingdom of God. It concerned him to think that the people who were supposed to be preaching the only message that Jesus preached had not embraced it. He called it "the only message that Jesus preached" because he said Jesus did not spend all His time preaching about being born-again, but He preached the Kingdom of God. Jesus said, "I must preach the kingdom of God … because for this purpose I have been sent" (Luke 4:43 NKJV).

Jesus told His disciples to preach the same message of the Kingdom (Matthew 10:7). John the Baptist, who prepared the way for Jesus, preached that the Kingdom was at hand (Matthew 3:1-2). Dr. Myles said we must preach the message of the Kingdom because in it you find all other things, such as freedom of nations, justice, fairness, righteousness, and law. All these are found in the Kingdom.

Dr. Myles Munroe did not believe there is something called "secular." I hope that I can represent him well in his analogy or in trying to analyze things on his behalf. I know he was very much against the idea of saying when I'm at church it is sacred and when I'm working as a policeman, teacher, sportsman, or whatever, it is secular.

In Dr. Myles Munroe's mind, there was no secular and no sacred. He said that the message of the Kingdom encouraged us to go out into the world and teach the nations. He defined "nations" as ethnos—the different groupings of people, not just countries like South Africa, America, England, Kenya, Zambia, and Zimbabwe. He said we must go into the ethnos, which is all the different groupings of people. Go into the sports world, go into the medical world, go into the business world, go into all these different worlds, and make disciples in those worlds. Do not run away from these worlds; you must confront them and mix with them.

Dr. Myles Munroe had a unified vision for the ministry. He did many things, but he had one vision: Transforming Followers into Leaders and Leaders into Agents of Change. Addressing the Bahamas Faith Ministries fellowship in 2013, he said they had accomplished the first part of the vision, which was to transform followers into leaders. They were now going to focus on the next phase of the ministry, which was to transform leaders into agents of change.

Dr. Munroe had changed gears and he spent the last three or four years of his life challenging and advising the Bahamian government. It was during this phase of shifting focus onto transforming leaders into agents of change that he set up a committee at the church to look at the legal issues of the country. Before a Bill could be signed into law, the government would invite inputs from various quarters, including Bahamas Faith Ministries. A piece of legislation would not just be passed without the ministry's input. This process gave Dr. Munroe the peace of mind that they were handling important matters in his absence since he traveled so much. The Bahamian government took his advice seriously. He was one of the few Bahamian citizens to have spoken in parliament on leadership. He addressed the entire government on governance issues.

Myles Munroe would have loved to see his church in the Bahamas continue to become a local church with a global focus and mission to transform the world. At the same time, it should maintain its leadership authority and status as a moral compass in that nation. I believe that Bahamas Faith Ministries continues to champion that unified vision today after senior pastors, Dr. Dave Burrows, and his wife, Angie, took over the reins of leadership at the passing of Dr. Myles and Ruth Munroe, and Dr. Richard Pinder, in November 2014. Pastor Dave was part of the founding group that partnered with Dr. Munroe to launch BFMI. Dave Burrows and Myles Munroe met at Oral Roberts University and forged a close relationship that continued until the visionary's passing. I know that

Pastor Burrows is truly knowledgeable and would be sensible enough to change the style but not touch the vision. Vision is superior to style, which is a personality issue. There is no doubt that Dr. Myles Munroe wanted Bahamas Faith Ministries to go beyond being just another local church to one with a global vision. In the context of the Bahamas, BFM would remain a custodian of good governance and moral leadership in the country and around the world.

The Bahamas is a country where the Bible is the authority. Anytime Dr. Munroe challenged the government, it was always based on the preamble of their Constitution which states that the Bahamas should be governed according to the principles of the Bible. That gives the church a lot of power in the Bahamas because when you talk about biblical statutes and principles you are not speaking a foreign language, but the language of their Constitution.

The impact of Bahamas Faith Ministries, having a unified vision, cannot be underestimated. The founding group initially consisted of Dr. Munroe, Dr. Richard Pinder, Henry Francis, Dr. Dave Burrows, and their wives, and it later included Pastor Jay Mullings and several other early leaders of the ministry. They formed BFM in the early 1980s. Pastor Dave Burrows was the youngest of the founding group and held the position of Youth Pastor until he was appointed as Senior Pastor.

He is also known as a family specialist and has written at least seventeen books, including Kingdom Parenting, co-written with Dr. Munroe. I would say Pastor Dave understands the heart of the ministry and its foundational principles and precepts better than most. That vision is what makes the BFMI church unique. While it is up to him whether to follow the founding vision, I believe he recognizes the importance of continuing to build on it.

The other founder, Pastor Henry Francis, spent over thirty years in Finance and Banking in the Bahamas. He has been a committed leader in the ministry in charge of the finances. Pastor Francis is Vice President of the BFMI Board of Governors. He was Dr. Munroe's brother-in-law as he married his eldest sister, Sheila. Dr. Richard Pinder was also family of Dr. Munroe as he married Mama Ruth's sister, Sheena. She still lives in the Bahamas and is a great teacher and wonderful woman of God.

Myles Munroe believed that a unified vision in the Kingdom includes doing business. He was a member of different Boards and was involved in several organizations, including Bahamas Faith Ministries, Myles Munroe International, and International Third World Leaders Association. He spoke at corporations under his company called Leading Edge. The Munroe Group of Companies in the Bahamas mostly handles family-owned properties. When Dr. Munroe was not using his private jet, people could charter it through his company, Diplomat Aviation. He was diligent and transparent in all his dealings.

Train Up a Child

Dr. Munroe and I spent considerable time discussing growth strategies and plans for the organization. During one such conversation in 2013, I spoke of establishing a formal school that includes Kingdom principles in the curriculum. We discussed possible names for the school, such as Myles Munroe Educational Systems or simply Myles Munroe Academy. The school would follow a formal private school curriculum, while also teaching on leadership using his books as reference material. Myles Munroe believed that ideas should be institutionalized. That is why education must be part of his vision to deliver oppressed people. He always said that the way to deal with oppression is to bring light into the darkness. That is education.

I always liked those discussions, particularly when we were at Dr. Myles' home in the Bahamas. The same man who had just been teaching for an hour or two was always prepared to be present and give you his attention. He was always himself and happy to teach about life. I think he would have wanted us to continue to impact the Third World countries. He would have liked his organizations to maintain a strong focus on leadership development around the world and not just in one place. I think he would have loved to see his team of mentees and disciples band together and still go out in his name to do mighty exploits. Mostly, I think he would have loved to have his books become institutionalized. When you put all those books together, they form a foundational education system that can empower people to become responsible citizens of their own countries and communities. He would have loved for us to continue being involved in communities where followers are transformed into leaders who become agents of change.

> He would have loved to see his team of mentees and disciples band together and still go out in his name to do mighty exploits. Mostly, I think he would have loved to have his books become institutionalized.

In 2010, a prominent broadcasting group in South Africa launched an initiative called LeadSA. It aimed to encourage the public to "celebrate the achievements of the country while taking responsibility for its problems and challenges." I think Dr. Munroe would have loved for the Bahamas to have this kind of concept, run by concerned Bahamians. Such an institution could agitate change and keep challenging corruption in the country and leadership. It could align with the BFMI church to continue Munroe's work and ensure that the Bahamas becomes what God intended it to be. I believe that some of Dr. Myles Munroe's mentees in the Bahamas, or any other country for that matter, are well suited to lead an initiative like that. One name that springs to mind is Dr. Kendal Major, a prominent dentist, and former Speaker of the House of Assembly. Many other capable citizens could pick up the baton of leadership. This is what Dr. Myles Munroe was about. He was always prepared to challenge anything he knew was wrong and that violated God's will and plans for the nations.

Try New Things

Myles Munroe wanted people to learn from him then apply that learning for themselves and teach it to others. If you had read one of his books, for example, The Principles and Benefits of Change, he wanted you to personalize it. He wanted you to absorb that information and when you had practiced it enough, he wanted you to teach it. He expected all his disciples to become teachers and transfer those lessons to the next generation or others he couldn't reach. He always said there were people we could reach that he could not. We should impact those people and empower them with what we have received.

He expected and instructed us as mentees to write books. He always said we must write books. Some people in our circles did and he wrote the Foreword. I made a slow start as an author because I was too busy assisting him at the time. However, we did begin to co-author a corporate handbook, Thank God it's Monday. He believed that that book would have a global impact. He expected me to teach on it and said it would help people around the world.

He expected us to understand the Kingdom of God in a way that we could teach it. He felt that there were too few ministers teaching on the Kingdom of God because pastors are supposed to understand it but do not. He would have expected us to continue to spread the word, write our books, and get involved in our communities and politics. He felt we needed to get involved in the affairs of our nations and our cities. He also would have wanted his DVDs and books to continue to speak to people.

Uphold the Standard

Myles Munroe's books are still available in stores and so we are now focused on building schools that will carry on his vision. I envisage schools with different campuses in key provinces of South Africa and eventually spreading to countries we had visited in Africa. Let's say our first school is in Gauteng province. I then see this campus giving birth to one in Kwazulu-Natal, followed by campuses in Limpopo, North West, and Mpumalanga. I believe those four provinces will be quick to welcome a school that is based on Myles Munroe's teachings. However, the School Head Office will be where the vision bearers are. We will make it one unified school with the various campuses as satellite colleges. We plan to target all the African countries we visited.

This vision of establishing schools needs substantial investment. However, it cannot be at the expense of the trust we have developed with high-profile leaders. A reasonable person should stay within reasonable confines and expectations. I respect relationships and want to use them for what matters. You want to make sure you don't involve a king or Head of State in something frivolous. Take Swaziland for example. Dr. Munroe passed before he could teach the different spheres of government in the country, although he already had the mandate to do so. You should never underestimate the power, knowledge, and presence that Dr. Myles Munroe can still bring to a place through his mentees. While he is irreplaceable, we still have a team of experts that can teach leadership principles in ministry, business, or government. For example, we have Dr. Siphamandla Zondi who is a well-known professor of political science. He is an expert on African politics and has a similar style to Dr. Munroe whom he also learned from. I still speak on leadership and there are a few others who can do the same. The key is to be highly organized and ensure you deliver the promised benefits to the client. It can take years to build trust but only a moment to betray it.

One should take particular care when fundraising. You could go around using Dr. Myles Munroe's name to gain an audience with a president or king, and then be seen as an opportunist. Therefore, I am careful about raising funds from people we know and respect. You don't want anyone to think you are taking advantage of the fact that Myles Munroe is no longer around. Take the schools that we are planning to build for example. If I approach someone influential and ask for their support, I will only do so with a proper presentation that includes a plan of the school, the curriculum, and a list of things the school needs. When you are well organized, people will support your vision.

If I approach a king with the idea, he might not be able to build the school for us, but he could make sure the idea is incubated and the opportunity created for it to be fulfilled. The king may offer us some land on which we could construct school buildings. Some churches even have properties big enough to accommodate a school campus. You just want to make sure your thought process and paperwork are aligned. Then you can deliver a proper presentation to a hundred people at a time and enlist their support. A vision this large needs to have Infrastructure Development Partners because you can't run a school from a remote office; you need proper facilities where you have your own space with classrooms, sports fields, hall, etc. Once all that is in place you are positioned to achieve more. But it starts with a heart free of guile and an unwavering commitment to uphold the standard.

Be Ready to Lead

Dr. Myles Munroe believed we are all born to lead but we must become leaders. He believed we all have leadership capabilities and capacity. The capacity to lead is in each one of us but we must learn how to lead. You must become that leader. He believed that the purpose of leadership is not to maintain followers but to produce other leaders. He also believed that leadership is not a position or title but a function. Munroe believed that leadership is spiritual. That is why he wrote the book called Spirit of Leadership. He believed that leadership is an attitude. He said that an army of sheep led by a lion will always defeat an army of lions led by a sheep. He believed there is a spirit of leadership hiding in conviction, confidence, and attitude because leadership is an attitude.

Munroe often used the lion to illustrate his point. He said the lion is called the "king of the jungle" for a reason. The lion is smaller than the elephant, slower than the cheetah, and not the wisest animal around, yet commands respect. When a lion sees an elephant, it sees one thing—lunch! While others see something that could crush them with its feet, the lion sees possibilities. Myles Munroe believed that no group of people was born to lead others who are dumb. He believed that anyone could develop into a leader. That is why he called his book, Becoming a Leader.

Early on in my corporate career, I convinced the executives at the Auditor- General's office to invite Dr. Myles Munroe to address us. I think he was impressed after that meeting because he crouched and hoisted me onto his shoulders. He said to me, "You are greater than your position. Never doubt yourself. Look at what happened here. God has used you in this situation. These people didn't know me and so I probably would not have accepted their invitation. You are their leader because you are leading them. Never be impressed with others' titles and positions."

> Dr. Myles Munroe's goal was to transform people who were taught to think they could not be anything in life. His job was to deliver them through his timeless message of leadership.

Myles Munroe believed that you are born to lead in your gifting and purpose. When people talk about leadership, they are usually referring to positions and how to mobilize people and make them do what you want. That is what most books on leadership are about. Dr. Myles Munroe and several other experts on leadership had a different view; they were appealing to people's mindsets. The psychology of leadership is not about making people do things. He was attacking the mindset that says others cannot lead, as found in apartheid and other forms of racism and bigotry.

His goal was to transform people who were taught to think they could not be anything in life. His job was to deliver them through his timeless message of leadership. I think his book will remain relevant to many cultures and generations for decades to come.

I discovered the lack of a leadership mindset through my travels with Dr. Munroe to different countries. The problems that we think are ours alone are found all over the world. Third World people are everywhere because the Third World is also a mindset. Some of them inherited it from their forefathers who were themselves oppressed. The spirit of the oppressor continues to impact one generation after another. Dr. Myles Munroe always reminded us in South Africa to not be too tough on our government because it was only twenty years old. He called South Africa "adolescent," as we were not even in the youth stage yet. He said this because he was afraid that South Africa, like the Bahamas, was at risk of the oppressor coming back to rule the country. He was afraid that Black people could relinquish power through corruption and many other means. He wanted us to jealously guard the democracy and freedom that we have because it came at a cost. He anticipated things way before they happened. He knew that one of the things which is still a "time bomb" for South Africa is the issue of land. He said it many times.

Visionary leadership should first establish the vision of the country then establish the values of the country needed to support that vision. He warned us and helped us to understand what we need to look for in politicians.

He said we should not look for promises of water and electricity and stuff like that when politicians are canvassing for votes; we must ask about their vision for the country. The vision for the country is more important.

He understood South Africa very well. I think on many occasions he strongly asserted himself on those matters when meeting with the different levels of government in this country. He met all levels of government—local, provincial, and national. He always used to say that you must guard what you have. He taught us that there is a difference between a politician and a leader because a politician is thinking of the next election while the leader must think of the future generations.

We remember him for the many things he taught us, that he wanted us to continue with, and what he expected from us. I think his expectations were clear; he clarified those very well for all of us. Dr. Myles Munroe understood leadership. He said something about the fact that South Africa's ruling party, the African National Congress (ANC), was going to lose power. There would come a time when the ANC would lose power. They had seen this also in the Bahamas; the party of the founding father lasted for some years, but the next generation had a way different focus as they had never even smelled apartheid. He said you can ride the wave of freedom for twenty years and enjoy the fruits of those who had fought for freedom. Then there would come a time when people just did not care about who had fought for what. All they wanted to know was that equality, freedom, and opportunities were there. Munroe reminded us that we shouldn't forget those stories. I remember him telling former president Jacob Zuma that the schools should teach kids what it took for them to be there. No child should leave school without understanding the price that was paid. He said it must be a compulsory subject, regardless of whether they were doing mathematics, science or whatever; everybody should be made aware of their history because if you don't have a sense of your history, you don't appreciate the future. He said the story should be told.

Preach the Kingdom

Dr. Munroe felt that any ministry that is not playing a role in society is irrelevant. Kingdom leadership should impact society and make its presence known. An effective church is one you cannot ignore. A Kingdom-based church should be effective. He felt strongly about that. Understanding the Kingdom's message is important to the liberation of people in different religions, including Christianity. He felt that the Kingdom of God should be the main or only message of the church. That is why he said he did not even preach about the Cross or the Blood of Christ; those are the means, but the end is the Kingdom. He said those are not even the good news; the good news is the message of the Kingdom of God. He respected the Crucifixion, he respected the Blood, and he could preach about them. He understood those principles but said we should not be lost in the means and forget about the end. The end is the Kingdom of God because although Jesus came to redeem us, it did not end there; it was redemption for restoration. Restoration means restoring our original state as found in Genesis chapter 1 where God made man in his image and likeness and gave us dominion over the fish of the sea, birds of the air, and so on.

He wanted us to have dominion over the earth. The death of Jesus on the cross salvaged that dominion mandate for man to go back to his original state. According to Myles Munroe, no restoration is bigger than the restoration of man back to God's original intention for us.

Restoration is not so much about getting a job or coming out of poverty; it is about you coming out of the shell that culture, apartheid, and colonialism put you in. Restoration is returning to what God wanted you to be—someone of authority reigning on earth with Him. Our focus is not even on heaven. Heaven was never Dr. Myles Munroe's focus. He said he had no control over heaven and that God gave him rulership and dominion in the earth. This is where we are to change the lives of people.

People must become the best they can be here. You receive a ticket to heaven when you accept Jesus and are saved. Your eternal future is settled when you are born-again. However, the mandate of mankind can only be exercised on this earth. Citizens of God's Kingdom should find practical ways of discipling the kings, princes and princesses, presidents, and ministers of government. That was his bone of contention. The church is ineffective and irrelevant. The church is administering what is not required. The church is scratching where it is not itching.

Whenever we address people, we must always remember to tell them about their Dominion Mandate because that is the main message. God's purpose for humanity is that we dominate earth on His behalf. God doesn't live here; He lives in heaven and sent us here to become His ambassadors and to represent Him. That is the fundamental message. The King sent His ambassadors to a distant territory called earth so He could colonize it with heaven. Those on earth could think like heaven.

The earth would have the culture of heaven, the mind of heaven, the style of heaven, the language of heaven, and the mannerisms of heaven so it could have the attitude of heaven. Many Bible schools don't put it that way. It is a simple concept to grasp but they make it difficult. Dr. Myles Munroe taught me that when I preach, my foundational book should always be the New Testament with the Old Testament to support it.

Complete Your Assignment

I think the world needs to learn about servanthood. I believe it is part of our Dominion Mandate. People need to know what success is and learn the keys to personal success. They need to be aware that God introduced mankind to the planet and that we are different from animals. People must learn to embrace the concept of humanity and not just define others as Black, White, Colored, or Asian. God has only one race that Dr. Myles Munroe knew of—the human race.

I want people to know that we are different and that we are different for a purpose. We are different so I can benefit from your difference, and you can benefit from mine. I want the world to learn that God is a God of justice, and He has no favorite races. Even the people we consider worthless are highly valued in God's economy. I want every human being on the face of the earth to know that they are important, no matter their background, race, or culture. That person, regardless of who they are, was created in the image of God. When I treat someone badly, I must remember that I'm ill-treating God's image. How can I say I love God when I hate people who are made in His image?

If you want to be effective as a Kingdom ambassador, you need to see things as God sees them. For example, most people measure success in terms of the things they acquire. Some pastors regard success as the number of members their church has, how big the building is, and so on. But the reality is that success is not measured by those standards. Success is when you become what God sent you to become. You are successful when you fully realize and express your Kingdom Mandate. Notice that I didn't mention any car, I didn't mention any house, I didn't mention any clothes or any amount of wealth. I'm speaking about God's purpose—His Kingdom Mandate for your life. God will only say to you, "Well done good and faithful servant" when you have done what He sent you to do.

The measure of your success is not about how successful you are but how faithful you are in your calling. That is particularly important. You measure your success according to how you have done what you were supposed to have done in the way God expected you to do it. I'm reminded of Jesus when He said, "I have brought you glory on earth by finishing the work you gave me to do" (John 17:4 NIV). Jesus gave the Father the report that He had completed His assignment.

Many believers say that they are glorifying God when they sing in the choir or are worshipping in church. However, that does not necessarily mean we are doing His will for our lives. You will only bring glory to God when you have done what you were supposed to do. That is true success.

I want the world to know that I had a mentor who made me what I have become. I want the world to know that I was blessed to have that heritage and to know what that heritage is. I want the world to know that you may come from a village, but the village doesn't define who you are.

My Life and Times with Dr. Myles Munroe

You can be a boy from Manamani village and still have an impact on the globe.

I also want the world to know that it is not just about you getting an education but being educated in line with your God-given purpose and then becoming successful in the pursuit of that purpose. Our schools are not teaching kids to become something in life. They just give them book knowledge. They don't graduate as leaders in a particular industry or are ready to do a particular vocation. They just teach them math and say, "You'll figure it out when you get to high school." But in high school, they say you'll figure it out when you get to university! Wouldn't it be wonderful if kids knew at an early age that they were born to solve all kinds of problems? We just need to teach them how to discover the God-given talents and gifts trapped within them. That is the main thing. If the church can't do that, it is irrelevant. A church is ineffective if it is just collecting offerings and tithes and not teaching the fact that you are a king functioning under the King of kings. We are to impact the world with

> The measure of your success is not about how successful you are but how faithful you are in your calling.

the culture of heaven and make known its intentions, will, and statutes. Any church not doing that is failing in its Kingdom mandate.

Earn Their Trust

I realized there are very few people who knew Myles Munroe well enough to be able to tell his story. I felt I could write his story on his behalf because I knew him so well. I understood his vision and passion. He once made a statement that humbled me very much. I would not have believed it had the person just told me verbally and not offered any proof. Rwandan author, business consultant, and speaker, Hubert Sugira Hategekimana, who was one of Dr. Myles's mentees in the mentoring program, came to me with a recording where Dr. Munroe told the mentees at a meeting that if you wanted to know his heart you had to visit South Africa and listen to Charlie Masala. Dr. Munroe said I was the only person who could speak on his behalf in his absence. I wanted to believe he was talking about people in general, but I think he meant it as a statement of fact outside of his family. He was speaking in the context of his ministry and ITWLA, which his children were not involved in at the time.

He gave some background on why he could trust me and why I was central to his ministry and the journey we walked together. That was when he came up with a concept called "abandonment," saying I was the only person he'd met who could truly abandon himself for his vision. He said that you are not ready to pursue any cause until you abandon yourself for the cause. That was a special endorsement and acknowledgment, and he repeated the same sentiments in many public platforms where he taught on servanthood. He had, however, told me previously that he thought God had him in mind when he created me. Those words will always be incredibly special to me.

Many people claim to know Dr. Myles Munroe because they had sat with him here or there. I came to believe I could qualify to write his biography because of the things he said about me and the fact that I had spent a lot of time with him. I might not be as mature/holy as he was, but I know a lot about his heart, disappointments, and vulnerabilities. He was exceptionally strong in the faith.

Chart a New Course

I believe that the future of Myles Munroe's organization rests in us doing what he would have expected us to do—continue to learn, teach, and impart but also institutionalize the material he left behind. The future is in making sure his resources can keep on talking to people in his absence. The way to do that is through books, both print and electronic versions, videos, and more importantly, institutions—the schools that we are to build. We can ensure Munroe's books continue to reach the different parts of the world. I think that will make the roots go even deeper. The institution will outlast all of us. The institution will go further perhaps than what the foundation can go. A school keeps on teaching. Even after a hundred years and we are long gone, the material has improved and become the culture of the school. So, every child who goes through the school will emerge more powerful than those who went before.

Now that Myles Munroe is gone, we can also keep speaking to people by generating resources of our own. We can reach people through television programs, but you can only do that to a point. The voice of Dr. Myles Munroe is not here, but we who were entrusted with his message are supposed to be the voice to go out and echo the message. In other words, Charisa Munroe must get her own voice, communicate what she has learned, and share what God reveals to her as she goes. Myles Munroe Jr. should do the same. It won't come out the same; we are all different. I must do the same and all those whom Munroe's message impacted must do the same. As I said, the principles remain the same although the delivery may vary.

Another important thing is that Dr. Myles Munroe had impeccable character. Therefore, anyone who continues his legacy must be beyond reproach. This is no easy feat as we were not raised like him and are not at the level he was. Still, we must do our best to represent his vision and legacy well. One way to do that is to build institutions that develop children into leaders. A school like the one we are building will help develop a post-matric course on leadership and design a unique Bible school that teaches the message of the Kingdom. That is important. His books contain those teachings, but we also know them because he taught them to us. There will be day students but also boarders housed in hostels on campus. We want to make sure that when they leave that place, the learners are ready to lead and have discovered their own areas of leadership and spheres of influence. That for us is a non-negotiable outcome. The school will transform many lives and shape destinies because it will be founded on

Kingdom principles. We are going to build leaders who will graduate from these schools with the desire and ability to change the world. I want that campus to be up and running seamlessly before I turn fifty. Then we will add a Kingdom-focused Bible School. It is particularly important because it will produce students who are Kingdom- focused and not just theology-minded.

I am actively working on bringing this vision to life. Plans are underway for a central office to soon establish the Munroe Institute which will go a long way in the goal to institutionalize Dr. Myles and Mama Ruth's work.

Find Your Calling

I'm driven by the need to help humanity find its place in the world. The discovery of purpose drives me. I want to help people discover the reason they are on the earth. I want to be satisfied that they know they came here for a purpose and that they can fulfill it. My purpose is to help other people find their purpose. That servanthood is my biggest driver. That is why meeting Dr. Myles Munroe was so important for me; my purpose in life became clear after I met him. I worked with him and gave my time to him because I knew he was operating under a higher purpose, which was to teach the world Kingdom principles, purpose, and leadership.

Dr. Myles Munroe said he wanted to work with people like me because I was self- motivated. He was an empowering leader who didn't interfere with the day-to-day administrative aspects of the organization. He had no time for micro-management. I owned his vision because my vision was to catalyze his work. That is the working relationship we had. He never doubted that when I suggested something, I was suggesting it because I had him in mind. Anytime I approached him with an idea, he always knew it was to support the bigger picture, which was his work. Many visionaries do not understand this principle. The relationship between Dr. Munroe and I illustrates the relationship between the visionary and the people who help carry the vision.

People need to understand that when they help the bigger vision take place, they are not on the losing end; it is simply part of the value chain.

When I did what I did best it helped catalyze Munroe's work. I was not speaking at the events when we went all over Africa, but my efforts enabled Dr. Myles Munroe to do what he had to do. That is why he always said he believed God created me with him in mind.

Aim High

God's purpose for our lives is linked to a broader purpose. My support of Munroe's vision helped to realize a vision beyond the visionary. We both knew what he lived for and what he wanted to accomplish. That agenda is still as powerful today because we can teach it to the next generation. The planned school is going to be a vehicle to get that done. My passion is to continue the vision he lived for to help people discover who they were born to be. Our job is to start a fire in them so they will have a burning desire and the tenacity to accomplish their God-given purpose.

This is easier said than done as Dr. Myles Munroe is difficult to replace. You need a bunch of people, a council, a whole community to accomplish everything he did. It is difficult to find someone who can operate at that level and impact the world the way he did. I draw on his wisdom in his absence whenever I'm faced with a situation, need to decide something, or understand certain concepts. I thank God for technology because we still have his CDs, DVDs, and books we can refer to. Even though he is no longer here, I can still hear his voice because I worked closely with him for so long. Myles Munroe always had something to say about any topic.

Given how tough it is to replace Myles Munroe, I am not going all out to try and find a replacement. I trust that God is working everything together for our good (Romans 8:28). I understandably have different relationships with different men of God, but Munroe's books contain enough inspiration to keep me going for the next fifty years!

If I meet someone who can play a specific role, praise the Lord. Meanwhile, I won't look to my pastor or anyone else to play the role that Myles Munroe played in my life because that would be unfair.

> Given how tough it is to replace Myles Munroe, I am not going all out to try and find a replacement. I trust that God is working everything together for our good.

Myles Munroe was dedicated to turning followers into leaders and leaders into agents of change. And that is something all of us, including me, must do. You can serve someone all your life but what happens when they pass on unexpectedly? It is up to each of us to pick up the mantle of leadership. We will still be serving the vision but in a higher capacity. One of the greatest ways we can honor Dr. Munroe's memory is to transform from being a follower into a leader. Dr. Myles prayed for me many times and he always said that I would become greater than he was. I still live to see that. With God's leading, it is possible. Jesus said that those who believe in Him would do even greater works than He did (John 14:12).

Myles Munroe became far more than what the average person becomes because he was the product of many things. Proper upbringing, discipline, and getting to know the Lord at a young age are among the key factors in this. By the age of thirty, he was already advising the elders in his country! I believe nothing is impossible with God and that is why I think the devil doesn't like me. If I become just ten percent of what I am meant to become, I will be a danger to his kingdom.

Be Humble

Myles Munroe taught us to humble ourselves but still know who we are. He taught us to operate with knowledge in humility. Another thing I learned from him was to always be ready for anything and be able to teach at a moment's notice. I am a good teacher because my mentor was a good teacher. This is without a doubt part of the heritage that I got from my dad, Dr. Myles Munroe. Without warning, he would hand me a microphone in front of thousands of people and just say, "Hey Charlie, please tell them about the books that we brought." I got used to the idea of always being ready because he expected it of me. He would say, "Learn what I am teaching you.

> I can teach because I had the best mentor anyone could have. Even my pastor and the church acknowledged the fact.

When you have learned what I'm teaching you, understand it, absorb it, and own it. Because only when you own it can you teach it." He also told me many times, "You know, Charlie, you could be a pastor any day. With the knowledge that you have, you won't be an average pastor. You don't need Bible school. What I have taught you is enough to enable you to teach others." I understood what he meant by that. When you understand the Kingdom of God and the Kingdom message you don't need anything else. I could still attend Bible school and learn the history of the Bible and all that. But I think he meant that mentorship had given me the right foundation and I was equipped to be an effective speaker and teacher.

When you know the bigger picture, you will never confuse the details. I see this all the time. Whenever my pastor put me on the spot, I could deliver what he asked of me. Let's say he approached me and said, "Charlie, I apologize for not asking sooner, but can you do something for me at short notice?" I would have no problem with this because Dr. Munroe taught me that if I focus on the bigger picture and understand the principles, I don't have to worry about the details. Most pastors prepare a message to teach but it doesn't work like that for us. We have been taught principles, and every other thing you are going to teach is embodied in these principles. A principle provides the structure under which all these other things are housed.

You can put me in a corporate meeting, and I will be able to share key principles without having to open a Bible or needing to quote Genesis Chapter One. Put me in front of a group of kids and I will be able to use the same principles but styled for comprehension. Give me couples and I will still use principles to address the issues of married people. I think what most Bible teachers lack is the principles. They consult the Bible to find facts they can give the people on a Sunday but have no foundation upon which to build those facts. That's why they end up shouting to the point they believe the more they shout the more anointed they are.

I can teach because I had the best mentor anyone could have. Even my pastor and the church acknowledged the fact that I have an unusual anointing and ability to teach. For example, my pastor once told me on Wednesday that he wanted me to preach that Sunday. The problem was, we were going with our wives to a wedding in Limpopo on Friday and only coming back Saturday night. I still had to deliver a sermon as if I had the whole weekend to prepare. I learned this from Dr. Munroe by observing him as he moved effortlessly from one meeting to another, addressing different topics and different audiences, from students to government leaders, politicians to company management. One man addressing different people and making every meeting count for that audience. That is a big lesson I learned from him.

Myles Munroe taught me confidence. He said to me, "When I call you up, I'm calling you up because I know you can do it. It shouldn't be a question in your mind whether you can do it or not, otherwise, I wouldn't have called you." He always said that when you teach always tell your story because you have the authority to address people's lives in your story. Nobody can argue with your story because nobody knows your story better than you and nobody can tell it better than you. You should tell your story.

Leave a Legacy

The church's job is to prepare the Bride, but it is not doing that effectively enough. The church should be training and refining the gifts within the body of Christ, including among the youth. That is why I began working on a book called Seventeen Mistakes That Young People Make. Having delivered sermons in the church at my pastor's invitation, I have also addressed our youth conference. The pastor said my teachings were powerful and so I decided to collaborate with some of the youth to compile the content for the book. It is the kind of book that a youth ministry can pick up as a manual because it will teach them Kingdom principles. It will help young people to discover their potential. It will assist them in decision making, choosing the right friends and mentors, and stuff like that. There will also be sections on business development and entrepreneurship. Young people learn by doing things. This book illustrates common mistakes that young people make and how to avoid them.

As I mentioned, one of the focuses going forward is building of the school. This is my focus. A lot of effort and energy, meetings, and time are required to get this project off the ground. I believe Dr. Myles Munroe would have loved to see this vision come to pass because it will impart Kingdom principles to where it is needed most—the next generation. We plan to begin as a primary school catering for Grade RR to Grade 7 and later expand our offering up to the matric level. The vision will ultimately find its fulfillment with the roll-out of branches across Africa and the addition of a Bible School.

As part of this vision, Xoli and I accepted the call to start a kingdom-based ministry in Centurion, South Africa. Kingdom Community held its inaugural service on June 6, 2021. Our ministry and Mission are based on Dr. Myles Munroe's principles and values: Teaching the message of the Kingdom and building Kingdom communities. Our Vision further reflects those values: Transforming followers into leaders and leaders into agents of change.

My prayer is that God will bless this work as we continue to teach people about the Kingdom of God, make disciples of the nations, and in the process honor the legacy of Dr. Myles Egbert Munroe and Mama Ruth Munroe.

PART 5

DR. MYLES MUNROE ATTENDS SOUTH AFRICAN PRESIDENTIAL INAUGURATION, MAY 24, 2014

The relationship between Dr. Myles Munroe and South Africa dates to 1990 when he met Nelson Mandela who was on his first visit to the Bahamas just after he was released from prison. His memories of his two meetings with Mandela, the firm handshake, and the conversation at a dinner table with him were cherished moments he spent with someone he considered his mentor. He often described his emotions as he toured the prison in Robben Island and as he lay on the very concrete floor where Mandela had spent much of his prison sentence.

Dr. Munroe extolled the virtues of character-based leadership and how rare that is to find in today's world. He emphasized the power of influence, without which a leader could not accomplish much. As agents of change, to make a difference, we must "Integrate, Invade, Influence, and Impact." Mandela demonstrated this through his life and paid the price for it. Dr. Myles believed that Mandela was not a politician, but a true leader. "We don't need politicians in leadership, but we need leadership in politicians."

Yet, Mandela had his critics; even in his death and as a human, he wasn't without flaws. His uncompromising determination coupled with an equally unconventional approach in challenging the racist government of apartheid endeared him to some world leaders of the time not viewed favorably by the democratic nations. However, his life in totality served as a testament to the power of conviction, determination, and the willingness to die for one's belief that the world could not ignore. In the end, many of the same world leaders who opposed him found themselves on the wrong side of history and later clamored to be associated with him.

Dr. Munroe's fitting eulogy to Nelson Mandela represented a memorial to an icon of leadership in our generation, a liberator, and statesmen for the history books. A life well-lived, and leadership exemplified through character and conviction. Nelson Mandela left a legacy that puts him in the class of world leaders like Mahatma Gandhi and Martin Luther King Jr., one that not only inspires but elevates the standard for new and aspiring leaders, not just for the nation of South Africa but the world.

Dr. Myles Munroe's love for South Africa was evident in the number of visits he made to the land each year, sometimes twice but in his final year he came here four times.

When President Zuma's Invitation to Dr. Myles to attend the Presidential Inauguration arrived, we realized it was clashing with our annual tour of the Holy land—Israel. We took the invitation seriously and therefore had to plan to break our tour for two days so we could travel from Israel to Johannesburg to be part of that important ceremony. We caught a flight from Tel Aviv's Ben Gurion Airport on the evening of

May 22, 2014, and arrived in Johannesburg the following day. We were received by the Minister of Agriculture and Fisheries at the time, Tina Joemat-Pettersson, who was later appointed as the Minister of Energy. She ensured our smooth movements at the Union Buildings where the Inauguration took place. The arrival of Dr. Myles Munroe at the Nelson Mandela Amphitheatre in Pretoria was a kind of showstopper; every politician, leader, and government official, including ministers, wanted to shake his hand. We spent the whole day at the Inauguration ceremony and then caught a flight back to Israel that evening. It was a great experience for Dr. Myles and me. Below is a media report that the Nassau Guardian Newspaper of the Bahamas published on May 28, 2014. It covered the inauguration where Dr. Myles met the who's who of government, politics, and business in South Africa, including the then Deputy President Hon. Matamela Cyril Ramaphosa.[11]

Bahamian leadership consultant and bestselling author Dr. Myles Munroe joined heads of state from over 30 nations as a special guest of the government of South Africa for the inauguration of President Jacob Zuma, 72, at the Nelson Mandela Amphitheatre in Pretoria.

Munroe was invited by the Office of the President after a lengthy meeting with the president before the elections in April. Munroe was welcomed to the historic event by the former wife of the late President Nelson Mandela, Winnie Mandela.

"Tell your prime minister, Perry Christie, that I await an invitation to return to The Bahamas to complete the final chapter between our nations," Mandela said. Munroe was then invited to be seated with the heads of state and government ministers as a special friend of South

> The energy minister served as Munroe's chaperone during the day of festivities. Munroe also met with South Africa's new Deputy President, Cyril Ramaphosa, the ANC's second-in-command

Africa. This year also marks the 20th anniversary of the free democratic new South Africa.

Zuma assumed his second term in office as president on May 24, following the African National Congress' (ANC) victory in the national general election on May 7. "Dr. Munroe was invited because he has been a valuable friend of South Africa for the past 20 years, first through his television programs that aired on the national South Africa Broadcasting Corporation (SABC) since 1994 and have inspired millions of South Africans with these powerful empowerment messages," said the new Minister of Energy Tina Joemat-Pettersson.

The energy minister served as Munroe's chaperone during the day of festivities. Munroe also met with South Africa's new Deputy President Cyril Ramaphosa, the ANC's second-in-command, who was appointed by Zuma to focus on running the economy and restoring investor confidence in the country.

The former union leader returned to the political fold last year after 16 years in the private sector, where he amassed a significant fortune.

About 40 African leaders and 4,500 dignitaries attended the inauguration, including former South African President Thabo Mbeki.

During his speech after the swearing-in, Zuma laid out his administration's priority agenda. "This second phase will involve the implementation of radical socio-economic transformation policies and programs over the next five years," he said.

"The structure of the economy will be transformed through industrialization, broad- based black economic empowerment and through strengthening and expanding the role of the state in the economy."

Munroe was scheduled to return to South Africa in August to meet with the president and his new Cabinet to discuss additional leadership training programs.

Dr. Myles Munroe, Mama Ruth, and Charlie with South African President
Jacob Zuma in 2014

PART 6

REFLECTIONS FROM CORPORATE AND MINISTRY COLLEAGUES

Sponsoring Charlie Masala's Trip to the Bahamas for a Leadership Convention

Charlie joined my management team in December 2000 as HR manager. His interview for the job took many hours as we discussed life, family, leadership, our vision, purpose, and religion. As a result, Charlie's car was locked in a parking facility all night, but I was so fascinated with this young man that I let him use my car to travel home. I ended up begging for a ride home in my car!

I was captivated with Charlie as a colleague and friend and managed to convince the directors of our bank to later that year sponsor his first trip to the Bahamas for a leadership convention. This was the end of Charlie's banking career as he instantly answered the Lord's calling and devoted his life to serving His Kingdom. The late Dr. Myles Munroe took charge of Charlie's development and as one of Dr. Myles' most trusted leaders, he became the Managing Trustee of South Africa-based Myles Munroe Foundation. I was privileged to act in a consulting role on the Board of Trustees, through which I met Dr. Myles and worked with both him and Charlie on many South African projects. After the tragic death of Dr. Myles, his wife, Ruth, and others, on November 9, 2014, Charlie continued to industriously build and expand the Munroe legacy in South Africa and globally. He also became well-known as a motivational speaker and teaches Kingdom principles regularly at universities and corporations.

Mr. Francois P. Saunders
General Manager: Banking Sector
South Africa and Botswana

A Young, Youthful, and Fearless Charlie Masala

Having had the distinct and fortunate honor to be part of Dr. Myles Munroe's International Third World Leaders Association (ITWLA), my husband and I were privy to meetings with some distinguished leaders and people from across the globe. I can't quite remember when I first met Charlie Masala, but I will never forget him—the young, youthful, fearless Charlie.

Dr. Myles Munroe was our friend, confidant, fearless leader, and powerful speaker, but Charlie grew to be his son, his adopted son, whom we all knew and loved. We were so happy to know both. Dr. Munroe loved Charlie, as Charlie endeared himself to him. The sentiments were mutual. It was evident that Dr. Munroe was pouring into the life of Charlie, and Charlie was a willing recipient.

In my view, Charlie held Dr. Munroe in high honor and regard as God's anointed servant, and the student was always learning from the teacher. The joy was seeing the young, energetic, aggressive Charlie with Dr. and Pastor Ruth Munroe. It was evident that Charlie had a determination to get the message of the Kingdom to the masses. I am assured that everything Dr. Munroe imparted to Charlie's life will impact the world. The message of the Kingdom will continue because of Charlie Masala.

Dr. Sylvia Jordan
Stateswoman, USA

Charlie was to Myles as Timothy was to Paul

Myles Munroe and I had a close relationship that began when he was a teenage student at ORU. I had the honor of being the speaker at the first annual conference sponsored by BFMI. I was the only speaker at that conference, held in March 1982. I also preached on Sunday of that week, when the group had its first worship service as a church. One of my highlights every year thereafter was to preach and teach at each conference and summit meeting.

I had the privilege of opening the door for Myles to minister in Africa by encouraging Ezekiel Guti to invite him to Zimbabwe. Thereafter, Myles' African ministry grew rapidly, and people from Africa began to attend the conferences in Nassau. Among them was a tall, quiet young man by the name of Charlie Masala.

When I first met Charlie, I recognized him as a disciple who wanted to learn all he could from the teachers, especially Myles. He didn't say much, but he listened intently. It was a blessing to see how Charlie grew from year to year, developing from a student/follower into a teacher/leader. I think that in many ways, Charlie was to Myles as Timothy was to Paul. Myles poured volumes of wisdom into Charlie's life until Charlie was saturated with that wisdom and with a zeal to share it. After that, there was no holding him back.

The time with Myles, learning from him and serving with him, was a preparation that he could not have received in a seminary. As a result,

Charlie developed into the energized and effective ambassador of the Kingdom of God that he is today.

Dr. Jerry Horner
Former Professor
Oral Roberts University, USA

Charlie Masala Introduced us to Dr. Myles Munroe

People work with people to realize greater heights in life and beyond. My family and the ministry had a rare opportunity to experience, feed, and be empowered through the grace God bestowed on Dr. Myles Munroe, Mom Ruth, and the Munroe Family.

This would not have been possible the way it unfolded were it not for the wisdom and good heart of Mr. Charlie Masala and his family. Although I already knew about Dr. Munroe, Charlie Masala formally introduced us to him in 2009 when our ministry hosted Dr. Munroe, becoming an annual event for the next five years. This started a transformative journey whose true value the world is yet to see.

Being close, I was able to observe a unique and special relationship between Myles Munroe and Charlie Masala. Dr. Munroe genuinely loved, trusted, depended on, praised, and openly acknowledged Masala's leadership qualities. He called him Charlie and regarded and treated him as a son. Charlie reciprocated through honor, excellence, and relentless commitment to serving Dr. Munroe, demonstrated in leading Myles Munroe International (MMI) in Africa, organizing some international trips for him, and particularly, playing a pivotal role in making the Israel events a great success.

Charlie opened doors for many of us to fellowship and learn personally from Dr. Munroe, among others, by including us in the entourage of trips in Africa. He showed his good heart and investment in the life of Dr. Munroe. On one of the trips, Dr. Munroe said, "You were created not just to exist but to live a fulfilled and significant life." Serving Dr. Munroe created fulfillment in Charlie's life and made the ministry of Dr. Munroe significant, successful, and impactful in Africa and elsewhere.

Dr. Munroe's children regard Charlie as their true brother, and Mom Ruth loved Mrs. Xoli Masala. In my considered view, if there is somebody in the ITWLA family who captured the message and could run with the baton from Dr. Munroe, it is Mr. Charlie Masala. I salute him for that great spirit of servanthood to another man. The Masalas and Munroes worked with one another, and together they realized greater heights.

Dr. Simanga Alex Tsela
Kingdom Embassy Centre
South Africa

Charlie was a Focused Student of his Mentor's training

I first met Charlie Masala at a Global Leadership Summit event presented by Missionary Statesman and Ambassador Extraordinaire, Dr. Myles E. Munroe, at the Diplomat Center in Nassau, Bahamas. As one who has been privileged to serve principal leaders in their quest to fulfill their God-given vision, enough cannot be said about those who give themselves to assist such visionaries. In the spirit and demonstration of such service is how I came to meet, appreciate, and admire Charlie Masala. I was honored to receive an invitation to join Dr. Munroe at a conference in South Africa. In his supportive ministry role, I observed firsthand how Charlie effectively and efficiently assisted Dr. Munroe as the latter traveled the world to train thousands of leaders.

Charlie's dedication, diligence, and loyalty were rare but vital qualities necessary for such specialized service to a global thought leader like Dr. Munroe. I watched Charlie labor tirelessly in his function of leadership, representing the Kingdom of God and his mentor at every level. Charlie exhibited competent, multi-tasking skills, along with very polished personal rapport with many different people ranging from airport ramp workers to high-level governmental officials. It was abundantly clear to me that Charlie was a focused student of his mentor's training. His attitude was consistently positive no matter the task. Perhaps Charlie's most admirable traits are his love, devotion, and honor toward God, Xoli, his wife, and their beautiful children.

Dr. Joseph Ripley
Body of Christ Church Intl.
United States of America

Charlie is a Son of Excellence

I met Charlie and Dr. Munroe in Nassau, Bahamas when first I attended the ITWLA leadership conference. I connected with Charlie quickly because he was among very few people from Africa so I could relate to him on a more personal level. However, I did not know who Charlie was to Dr. Munroe until I traveled with the team to East Africa in 2013. Charlie was the eyes, ears, and everything in between for Dr. Munroe on that trip to an extent I could not imagine. During the trip, I saw that all Dr. Munroe was doing depended on Charlie's efficiency.

Many people who have never been on a trip with Dr. Munroe in Africa will never appreciate what Charlie meant to him. Charlie was a son of excellence, the one who gave up all to serve his father's vision with not only a passion but a level of sacrifice that many people cannot fathom. What I saw with my eyes on that trip was confirmed by Dr. Munroe himself when one day he was discussing with me and other mentees what it took for him to trust someone.

He used Charlie as an example of the abandonment he looked for in people he could work with. He said that Charlie was the only person on earth that could speak on his behalf without first having to consult with him because he understood his heart. After that meeting, he advised us to go and spend some time with Charlie Masala in South Africa to understand Dr. Munroe's heart better. Charlie understood and embodied the principles of sonship—a decision one makes to submit to, serve, and honor a father figure, despite his imperfections.

Mr. Hubert Sugira Hategekimana
Author/Speaker
ITWLA Trustee

Charlie Submerged himself in the Spirit of Sonship

Dr. Myles Munroe spent about sixty years on earth before he was recalled to the home country. He spent his life studying the original message of Jesus and trained thousands of mentees around the world. Many of these mentees became his "sons and daughters." Over the years I had the opportunity to observe one of his sons, Charlie Masala. Dr. Munroe took an interest in all his mentees according to each of their assignments. He spent a lot of time with Charlie in South Africa and

222

groomed him into a leader who now touches many influential leaders from Heads of State to those that are in the field.

Charlie does what he does best because of his submission to the ideals, vision, and mission of his spiritual father, Dr. Myles Munroe. The trust that was established between them spilled over to the trust of their families. Today, Dr. Munroe's biological son, Myles Jr., and daughter, Charisa, spend much comforting family time with the Masala family because of this relationship over the years.

Dr. Munroe's organization, ITWLA, is successful, growing, and expanding as Charlie unconditionally applies the lessons he learned from his spiritual father, Dr. Munroe. Charlie Masala submerged himself in the spirit of sonship, contrary to the failing and hazardous leadership we have seen around the world for the past decade. He recognized while people may change, the laws of God never do. The biblical pattern for perfect generational transfer was seen over the years in their relationship. I have had Charlie at our house and church on a few occasions. I must say I genuinely enjoy his happy, jolly, and innovative personality around our community. I see the spirit of his father upon him and the continuation of the Kingdom of Heaven and its expansion through his personality and gifting.

We thank God for the example established and modeled by Charlie Masala and Dr. Munroe over the years. The success I saw in Dr. Munroe and his family is what I see in Charlie and his family today. There was truly a unique relationship between Dr. Munroe and Charlie Masala that moved him from being a mentee to being a son of this legend.

Dr. Pepe Ramnath
CEO and Speaker, Pepe Ramnath Intl. USA

Charlie Ensured that Dr. Myles and his Vision were Always Protected

Sometimes in life, our purpose connects us with individuals who hold the keys to our relationship with God and the world. That happened at a Third World Leaders conference in 1997, between Dr. Munroe, Charlie Masala, and me. Something supernatural happened. Myles Munroe and Charlie Masala joined in spirit and appreciation of each other's skills and talents.

The relationship grew as Dr. Munroe decided Charlie would be MMI's representative in South Africa. I recall when asked how he arrived at the decision, Dr. Munroe said, "Charlie has integrity, but more importantly he is my son. I love him and I can trust him." However, there was reciprocal love and respect when they were around each other. Dr. Munroe loved Charlie and his family. Every time he spoke about South Africa, he saw Charlie Masala as the hope for this new world he envisioned.

Most admirable was the respect Charlie displayed. Nothing had to be said. He knew what was acceptable to Dr. Munroe and took time to ensure he and his vision were always protected.

Dr. Patrick Rolle
Former Director at Bahamas Aviation
Consultant: Introspect Inc. Nassau, Bahamas

Level of Devotion, Love and Self-sacrifice for a Higher Calling

In 2008, Charlie Masala and Jerome Edmondson visited the church where I was fellowshipping in Emalahleni, South Africa, for an evening service. It was a different church experience that day for me as I felt drawn to them and exchanged contact details with Charlie. I researched him and found out he had a mentorship program to which I quickly enrolled. That was the beginning of my relationship with Charlie Masala. In 2009, I joined Charlie on a trip to the Bahamas for the annual ITWLA leadership summit and that is when I was introduced to Dr. Myles Munroe.

Over the years I continued a relationship with Charlie and got to learn about how he served Dr. Myles for over 20 years. I observed their relationship closely and there are simply no words to describe the level of devotion, love, and self-sacrifice for a higher calling. That is what Charlie did when he put aside his business to serve Dr. Myles full-time without any expectations or promise of anything. Over the years I watched how he served Dr. Myles with everything he had at a level I had never witnessed before. The closest comparison could be the relationship between Elijah and Elisha in the Bible.

I was equally amazed at how Dr. Myles reciprocated love and devotion to Charlie and his family to the point where he would entrust Charlie with everything when it came to organizing the ministry and all programs in Africa. The bond was that of love, family, and devotion to one another. This bond was evident in the many dinners and nights spent in private with Charlie and his wife, Xoli, my wife, Mpumi, and I, and the Munroes. It was an experience that transformed my life and family forever.

I will never forget the night that Dr. Myles, his wife Mama Ruth, and seven others transitioned in that unexpected plane crash. I was going towards the elevator to go downstairs at the hotel after hearing the news when Charisa came bursting out of the elevator alone, looking devastated and in tears. Out of all the people who were there that night she only asked for one person—Charlie Masala. It confirmed Dr. Myles' words when he said, "When you choose a successor, choose one that loves you because they will love and protect what and who you love."

Mr. Eric Mabuza
Mining Engineer, Speaker

A Young Lion Undaunted in Purpose and Intention

I met Charlie Masala in Nassau, Bahamas, in 2012, during the Global Leadership Summit hosted by The International Third World Leaders Association, chaired by the late Dr. Myles Munroe. As the meeting commenced, I saw Charlie walk in behind Dr. Munroe. Charlie's walk left no doubt that he was a young lion undaunted in purpose and intention. The following year, I traveled to South Africa with Dr. Myles and Pastor Ruth Munroe. Charlie and his wife, Xoli, were our gracious hosts and astute guides.

The level of commitment and honor Charlie exhibited, from arranging meetings to accommodation for Dr. Munroe was bar none. However, the most memorable moments were times of sage teaching and instruction shared between Dr. Munroe and Charlie—father lion to young lion, mentor to mentee.

Charlie's faithfulness to Dr. Munroe can be afforded the parallel of the disciples that "left all" to follow Jesus, and Charlie will likewise "receive a great reward." Charlie has since grown into a father lion and is mentoring young lions, as did his father, Dr. Munroe, before him. This is the "circle of life."

Congratulations on this book, Charlie! I know it will impact many lives!

H.E. Dr. April Ripley
Ambassador: Word of Life Ministries Intl, United Nations Geneva
Executive Trustee: International Third World Leaders Association
Chief Executive Officer: The Premiere Image, Inc.

Charlie has an Amazing Ability to Serve

"Who Are You Charlie...really?" When I met this servant-slave to Dr. Myles Munroe's Africa mandate, I was amazed by his ability to serve and know-how to serve with little to no coaching. Charlie, once we landed in Africa, knew what to do and as always, our entire agenda was planned. When I say planned, we didn't have a minute extra.

From the arenas with sometimes millions in attendance to a private plane to Swaziland or another African land to the safaris to watch massive lions eat, as Charlie had arranged for the feeding to occur when National Geographic Myles Munroe showed up! He loved some Myles Munroe and I loved me some Charlie Masala.

Mr. Jerome Edmondson
Entrepreneur Development Network
United States of America

Charlie has Committed his Life Unequivocally to Honor

Charlie Masala of South Africa is a long-standing covenant brother, with whom I had the honor of crossing paths through the amazing connection with the late Dr. Myles Munroe in Nassau, Bahamas, during an annual leadership conference. He is committed to his life's passion as a Kingdom motivational speaker across the world. I know him to be trustworthy, reliable, and a carrier of immeasurable knowledge in seeking to network with international leaders and expand the Kingdom Message.

Charlie has a plethora of experience in team building, accommodating strategic dialogue, and executing large conference agendas. He is an avid reader and an extremely knowledgeable individual whose organizational and management skills enable him to serve as a valuable voice to nations.

He has committed his life unequivocally to honoring God and his spiritual father and mentor, the late Dr. Myles Munroe. While serving as trustees of the International Third World Leaders Association, I had the opportunity to witness Charlie's extraordinary leadership and vision casting as the organization forged ahead into its future.

Although he has authored books, presented many sermons across international waters, and sat among earthly kings, Charlie's most treasured assets are his beautiful and multi-talented wife along with three adorable and bright daughters. Charlie is to be honored and recognized as a man of God and one who is constantly displaying a lifestyle of Kingdom takeover.

Dr. Martin L. Williams
CEO and Founder: Dreamkeepers Intl
Omaha, Nebraska, USA

Charlie was Loyal to the Vision Given to Dr. Myles Munroe

For a long time, I kept hearing Dr. Myles Munroe refer to Charlie Masala in his videos and seminars. I have not met him personally, but his name was constantly on Dr. Myles' lips. I began to form a picture of Charlie in my mind. To me, he was like the mother who took her sons to ask Jesus to allow them to sit at His right and left in glory. What a privilege!

I didn't even know that Charlie was from Africa. I always thought they both lived in the Bahamas. One day I was shocked at a meeting where they trained mentees. There was Charlie among the panelists! Dr. Myles mentioned him and introduced him to have come from South Africa. I said to myself, "Oh Lord, my God, Charlie is from South Africa? What did he do that qualified him to be with this man?" Having gone through Dr. Munroe's teachings, principles, and this level of exposure, I knew that Charlie must have paid the price to be so close to him. There was something about Charlie that made a way into Dr. Munroe's presence. Charlie must have sacrificed much to become his mentee. I know there were qualities and characteristics that Dr. Myles sought and admired in Charlie, or else he wouldn't have embraced him as he did. Charlie mastered himself to follow Myles Munroe.

Charlie is an intelligent person—a must for anyone who wanted to follow Papa Myles. Charlie, you have been a forward-looking person. I can tell you that you were not following Papa to "prosper" but to "become." I met Dr. Myles Munroe in 2013 in Lagos, Nigeria. We carved out plans for his coming to Northern Nigeria. I met face-to-face with Charlie Masala. I can say with all my heart that Charlie's leadership is not strange to me; it is like a continuation from where I stopped with Papa. I am looking at him as a living light.

He demonstrated true servanthood by becoming so loyal to the vision God gave Dr. Munroe. He did this by making room for him in Africa and

Asia. They needed each other for the big vision to be executed. Your thought of establishing for him a corporate park office was something that struck my heart; Charlie is different. The other view is his heart to serve Dr. Myles. There were so many logistical challenges involved—like distance, finance, and manpower—that one could have been tempted to quit serving him; it was up to Charlie and his family to make things happen. This was Charlie's initiative and not Munroe's instructions, his project, or even his sponsorship. Charlie has a heart to serve.

Charlie Masala sacrificed all, including family welfare, for Dr. Myles Munroe. He reminds me of Elisha and Elijah. He gave up everything else to follow a great man. It was total abandonment in service to Dr. Myles Munroe. Charlie's determination to see Dr. Myles prosper in his ministry brings me to the point that we must be faithful in another man's vineyard.

There were so many admirable things about Charlie's relationship with Papa:

* Knowing his position and respecting boundaries was a great lesson for me.
  He did not take advantage of nor abuse the relationship.
* His position in Myles Munroe's heart. Papa Myles had high regard for Charlie and so entrusted him with much. Munroe showed us how to transform people through relationships, love, and care. He brought Charlie into his own family and called him "son."
* Charlie's speech at the funeral. Out of all the nations, continents, countries, organizations, and leaders that Papa Myles touched, they chose Charlie & Xoli Masala to speak; it is the highest reward of followership. It exposed Charlie to the world. It reminded me of the scripture, *"This is my beloved Son, in whom I am well pleased. Listen to him!"*
* Finally, the legacy that Papa left behind has overtaken Charlie Masala. We see Myles in him. We see his spirit, attitude, intention, and passion in him. In moderation, he is to be larger than Papa Myles. When we look at Charlie, we see Papa. So, run! Run long and run to the finish. The baton is with you! Who is receiving it from your hands? Papa is watching you!

Dr. Uzzah Wado Naniyason
The Diplomat Centre
Kaduna, Nigeria

Charlie Remains a Son, Serving Dr. Myles' Family, Children and Ministry

I first met Amb Charlie Masala more than two decades ago with Dr. Myles Munroe. With the opportunity that he afforded our ministry to host Dr. Myles, we witnessed firsthand how Charlie served Dr. Myles—not for what he wanted to get from him but for what he wanted others to get and receive from him. Charlie served as a Son, not as a servant working for a reward.

Even years after Dr. Myles went to be with the Lord, Charlie remained a Son, serving Dr. Myles' family, children, and ministry. Charlie makes us understand why Paul told Timothy there was no one else like him in his life. For all seek their own thing. Charlie, your servanthood makes this scripture alive. I want to be a Son like you. I wish all my Sons would be Sons like you.

Your servant heart makes this book a living classroom. Congratulations on this workbook which will serve many generations to come.

Apostle Titus Sithole
General Overseer: Charity and Faith Mission
Mamelodi, Gauteng, South Africa

PART 7

VISION BEYOND THE VISIONARY

Near the end of Elijah's time on earth, he offered his assistant Elisha a gift: "What may I do for you, before I am taken away from you?" Elisha said, *"Please let a double portion of your spirit be upon me"* (2 Kings 2:9 NKJV). Elisha's request was to be considered Elijah's successor and to be "doubly blessed" with power in the prophetic office. Throughout 2 Kings, the many miracles Elisha performed confirm that he had indeed been granted a double portion.

Dr. Munroe always said in his teachings that the greatest act of leadership is *mentoring and training of successors* and that if your vision dies with you, you are a failure. Training and development of the next generation of leadership were among his main concerns. He believed that leaders are temporary and that the vision should outlive the leader. I believe that as Dr. Myles ascended on high, he dropped many mantles to many of us. I also came to accept that among the many mantles he dropped, one must have been for me. I have accepted the charge to teach the Kingdom and Kingdom leadership around the world. After his departure, I realized that I had been listening to him well because I can explain the Kingdom of God and teach its message with confidence and clarity with the necessary anointing. For the past six years, I have taught it around the world but only now have I truly embraced that calling. It was never my goal to follow Myles Munroe so that I could travel the world and teach like him. I believe this came more as a response to a call to preserve his legacy. Of course, God knew all this and had a plan figured out as people around the world still seek me out.

Over the years, I have heard people refer to me as an "Elisha" or "Joshua." It would be a shame for me to not emulate my father and build on what he taught. The year 2020 was a perfect opportunity for me to reflect and refocus. I now feel like someone who has taken an Oath of Office: "I, Lugisani Charles Masala, swear and promise to teach the Kingdom to protect and defend the integrity of the Gospel of the Kingdom of God."

It is a beautiful thing to behold that all the main organizations/entities that Dr. Myles Munroe founded and led (Myles Munroe International now called Munroe Global, Bahamas Faith Ministries International, and International Third World Leaders Association) are continuing, years after his departure. We never had a leadership crisis because he ensured there was succession planning. I am thoroughly pleased with the progress and success of Bahamas Faith Ministries under the capable leadership of Dr. Dave and Pastor Angie Burrows. I have had the privilege of working with Pastor Dave Burrows as I have hosted him on visits to South Africa for several years now.

Myles Munroe Jr. and Charisa Munroe-wilborn have also risen to the challenge and have been visiting South Africa on speaking visits. The two Munroe siblings founded the Myles and Ruth Munroe Foundation which is establishing the Munroe Institute.

Munroe Global continues to share the message of the Kingdom. Myles Jr. was also elevated to the position of Chairman of the International Third World Leaders Association. There is no doubt that both Papa Myles and Mama Ruth are rejoicing in heaven today over all these developments.

Dr. Myles Munroe said he didn't want His name on the buildings but in the hearts and lives of those he impacted so they could keep impacting others in the quest to transform followers into leaders and leaders into agents of change. He believed that all his mentees were to succeed him. He often used to pray that I would become greater than he was. Dr. Myles believed in his mentees. The greatest example of this principle came from the Master himself when He said, *"Very truly I tell you, whoever believes in me will do the works I have been doing, and they will do even greater things than these, because I am going to the Father"* (John 14:12 NIV).

Since the departure of Dr. Myles Munroe, I have been invited and traveled to teach in different nations including the Bahamas, United States of America, Indonesia, Philippines, Papua New Guinea, Nigeria, Kenya, Rwanda, Tanzania, Zimbabwe, Democratic Republic of Congo, Malawi, Gabon, and Cameroon, to name a few. The following accounts highlight my experiences on several of these trips.

Indonesia Mission

My first overseas speaking invitation was just after Dr. Myles departed. It came from Pastor Indri Gautama of the Apostolic Generation Church in the heart of Jakarta, Indonesia. Apostle Indri had been studying the

Kingdom message and following Dr. Munroe's teachings and we had been arranging for him to visit her ministry.

In July 2015, my wife and I traveled to Indonesia where I spoke fourteen times during the eight days we were there. It was a series of conferences involving Kingdom teaching, business development teachings, leadership, and youth and men sessions.

On that trip, we were joined by Eric and Mpumi Mabuza, Rendani Nedohe, and Ps. Susan Kingal from Papua New Guinea.

My schedule was so full that I was speaking three times a day. I even did a television series on the Kingdom of God which played nationwide for thirty days! However, I felt a special anointing and grace to teach and could handle the high-level, high-impact schedule. It reminded me of the intensity of meetings we used to have with Dr. Munroe. Apostle Indri Gautama prophesied that I would write books and teach around the world. She encouraged me to study further and package my work. The trip to Jakarta was such a great success that I was invited for a follow-up visit in 2016. Both trips were a great success. I was overwhelmed with the love that the Indonesian people showed me and how receptive they were to the message of the Gospel of the Kingdom.

> I felt a special anointing and grace to teach and could handle the high-level, high-impact schedule. It reminded me of the intensity of meetings we used to have with Dr. Munroe.

United States of America Mission

From 2015 to 2019, I conducted a few coast-to-coast tours of the United States, preaching the Gospel of the Kingdom. Some highlights include numerous teachings at the Body of Christ Church International led by Drs. Joseph and Marjanita Ripley in Atlanta, Georgia, Shake the Nations Conference led by Dr. Martin and Pastor Lynnel Williams in Omaha, Nebraska, Miramar Kingdom Community Center led by Dr. Pepe and Angela Ramnath in Miramar, Florida, Acts Church Ministries International in Dallas-Fort Worth, Texas, led by Dr. Darrell Wilson, Texas Women Empowerment Foundation Conference in Houston, Texas, led by Dr. Deavra Daughtrey, Resonate Church Service in Newaygo, Michigan, led by Pastor Paul Ruzinsky, and Champion Kingdom Center in Charlotte, North Carolina, led by Dr. Stacy and DeNae LeMay, among others. The message of the Kingdom is being preached far and wide!

Rwanda Mission

In September 2015, I got an opportunity to travel to Kigali, Rwanda, to address the Kigali Visionary Leaders Conference led by Ambassador Hubert Sugira Hategekimana. I also had a unique opportunity to be a keynote speaker at the Rwanda National Breakfast session attended by ministers of government, Supreme Court justices, and business leaders. I talked about Godly Leadership, and Kingdom Leadership transforming society. This was a high-level meeting and I was thankful for how our meetings with Dr. Myles had prepared me for these moments.

Nigeria Mission

In September 2015, I traveled to Yola, the capital city of Adamawa State in North-Eastern Nigeria, to address a conference on the theme of Kingdom Culture of Influence, led by Pastor Abraham Biyasa. This was one of the most intimidating experiences I have ever had because I accepted an invitation to travel to one of the most dangerous and unstable places on earth. I was under constant military and police supervision from my arrival at the local airport to my departure a week later. This place is not too far from Sambisa Forest where over 200 kidnapped girls have been held captive for years. Just two weeks after my visit, a marketplace was bombed and over 32 people were killed. My host, Pastor Biyasa, was happy that I came, and we remain great friends to this day.

In 2019, I traveled to Kaduna, Nigeria, at the invitation of Dr. Uzzah Waddo. Kaduna is the capital of Kaduna State, located in Northern Nigeria, with most of the population being Muslim. We had awesome meetings in two cities and addressed issues of the Kingdom as well as leadership development. I only spoke at the conferences; there was no sightseeing at all for security reasons as kidnapping is said to be common in the region. The meetings had great attendance and people were very appreciative and receptive. In all these places I was aware that they received me in Dr. Myles' name with respect, honor, and high esteem.

Papua New Guinea Mission

In July 2019, I traveled to Papua New Guinea (PNG) for a series of conferences at the invitation of an ITWLA Trustee and Regional Ambassador, Ps. Susan Kingal.

This was another high-level visit as it involved the highest office in the land, the Office of the Prime Minister. I spent my first week in the city of Lae. Here I addressed a youth conference attended by students from different institutions of higher learning.

The second week I moved to Moresby, the capital city of Papua New Guinea. There I spoke at multiple services in the Tabernacle of Prayer Church, following an invitation by Pastor Joseph Walters, a gatekeeper and spiritual father of PNG. Our host, Pastor Walter Kaumi, is a great man of God and was a marvelous host. I spoke about seven times at that ministry. This is the main church in the city and most prominent leaders, including the Deputy Prime Minister, fellowship there. The people and leadership connected very well with my ministry which made my week-long stay there very enjoyable. We had a great connection and have remained family.

Through a prominent public servant, Dr. Clement Malau, we were also able to meet both the Prime Minister and his deputy for a bilateral meeting. The Office of the Prime Minister arranged a live interview for me at the National Broadcasting Authority. Although the visit to PNG was a high-level one, it felt very natural for me as I was used to these kinds of visits with my Commander-in-Chief, Dr. Myles Munroe. I have watched him addressing heads of state on too many occasions for me to be intimidated. Following are some of the reports from that trip.

Kingdom Ambassador Mr. Charlie Masala Conducts Diplomatic Consultation with The Deputy Prime Minister Of Papua, New Guinea, The Honorable Steven Davis PORT MORESBY, PAPUA NEW GUINEA, July 11, 2019

Stepping forward in the footsteps of his predecessor, international leadership consultant, Dr. Myles Munroe, Mr. Charlie Masala was hosted by Deputy Prime Minister, The Honorable Steven Davis for a solution-focused discussion of how effective national leadership determines vision and accomplishes goals to benefit the lives of citizens.

A familiar avenue of engagement for Mr. Masala, government leadership consulting is a continuation of his ongoing experience as a key team member of Dr. Myles Munroe, who during the latter chapters of his life addressed Heads of State throughout the world on topics of leadership, character, vision, legacy, identity, and purpose. Munroe's stated mission involved enlightening governmental leaders—to transform followers into leaders, and leaders into agents of change.

This leadership consulting meeting today with a top-ranking government official marks a passing of the baton to Mr. Masala, now engaging in a role for which Dr. Munroe had groomed him for over two decades until Munroe's sudden passing in November of 2014.

Governmental leadership is entrusted to solve problems by identifying and strategically confronting challenges faced by those whom they serve. The Honorable Steven Davis is himself an accomplished leader, highly trained in the legal profession, and a promoter of education and reform programs for disadvantaged youth in rural Papua New Guinea.

In concluding today's consultation with the Deputy Prime Minister, Mr. Masala directed the government leader to specific resources of reading materials written by Dr. Munroe through which the author continues to provide training to future generations of leaders as part of his legacy.

Upon reflection on today's assignment, Mr. Masala humbly expresses his deep appreciation to his mentor, Dr. Myles Munroe, for providing him with the experience, knowledge, and confidence to step into this trusted role in supporting those who carry both the burden and honor of national leadership. Mr. Masala is most grateful to the International Third World Leaders Association, ITWLA, founded by Dr. Myles Munroe, for keeping Dr. Munroe's legacy alive as the founder's brothers, sisters, sons, and daughters continue to influence nations through leadership training.

Mr. Charlie Masala Addresses Fellowship of Industry Leaders in Papua New Guinea. Participating At Same Forum Was the Nation's Prime Minister, James Marape
PORT MORESBY, PAPUA NEW GUINEA, July 13, 2019

Mr. Charlie Masala, an international leadership consultant, delivered a message on the Burden of Freedom to a select fellowship of national leaders. Participating was also the Prime Minister of Papua New Guinea at a function hosted at the Hilton Hotel Conference Center last night.

Significant to the scope of this meeting was the participation of distinguished leaders of industry and network graduates, individuals of high impact, having been educated and deployed throughout key areas of the nation's economy. This fellowship identifies how to give back to their nation through their capacities as captains of industry.

During the gathering, Prime Minister James Marape, who rose to leadership as the country's former finance minister, put forth his vision for the nation of Papua New Guinea.

Prime Minister Marape was chosen overwhelmingly in May of 2019 to lead its citizens. Mr. Masala is uniquely prepared to address the issues facing this nation. During his lecture, he presented examples from his own country of South Africa in their struggles "to take everyone with us," noting the importance of training the population to improve opportunities for the marginalized. In this process, the role of education, both formal and informal, is key.

Mr. Masala states that education must be decolonized and no longer offered in a structure designed by former colonizers who had little interest in growing the indigenous people. In a lesson from the history of his own country that gained independence in 1994, he reminds leadership that when oppressors do not provide enough education for a people to self-govern, a population is being set up for failure.

In addition to reshaping education, Mr. Masala directs attention to the need for change in the legal systems and framework. He challenges leaders to review and revise as necessary the laws from former regimes that are not benefiting the people.

Most importantly, Masala appealed to leadership to consider how the identity held by the individual citizen impacts the nation. Masala observes that if a person is told for years that he is not good for anything, that is not good for anyone, and particularly that is not good for a nation. A person who sees himself like this cannot add value to the Gross Domestic Product (GDP) of the nation. What then is the call of leadership?

Leaders must emancipate, train, and teach every citizen that there is something they can do for themselves.

He concludes that this means that government cannot simply focus on a nation's economy; rather its leaders must look at the mental condition of the people. A man who lacks self-worth will, as a result, operate from low self-esteem and would lack confidence. But when a people are empowered with capacity and strategies, countries will not be the same again. Following Mr. Masala's remarks, Prime Minister Marape noted his appreciation to Mr. Masala for his insights from a passage in Genesis 1:26 that affirms the nature of man, his identity and his purpose, and how leadership can benefit from using this paradigm.

The Philippines Mission

In 2019, the Lord opened a door for me in the Philippines and I ministered in three of their cities. This was one of the most remarkable trips I have ever embarked on. I was visiting the Philippines for the very first time. I was able to visit and ministered in Manila for IKMA, led by Ambassador Redentor Du, Kingdom Talk in Tacloban City, led by Coach Ariel and Precy Arce, and the Davao Conference at Destiny Church, led by Pastors Roy and Rochel Oliveros. I also spoke at a pastors' meeting organized by MX3 founder, Ms. Gina Mendoza.

The visit to Destiny Davao was a highlight of the trip as I stayed there for a week. I was able to connect in a special way with Pastors Roy and Rochel Oliveros, as well as their team. This team has become my family and we have great plans for our cities and our people in Kingdom Development and Education. I love the Philippines and its people. The country has become my "home away from home." It was on this trip that I met one of my best mentees—Mr. Shern Tan. God has some big plans for the nation of the Philippines, and I am committed to playing my part.

Recognizing and Honoring the Gift

I have had numerous opportunities to speak locally in South Africa since 2014 and have experienced the interest and respect of ministers as well as corporate organizations. People note the fact that I served Dr. Myles Munroe and other ministries, therefore I am who I am not by accident. Serve your way to the trust of others and into a leadership position.

Dr. Basil Tryon, who worked with Dr. Myles Munroe and hosted him numerous times, was among those who recognized the apostolic and teaching gifts in me and became vocal about it. I have known him for over thirteen years and in that time, I have come to respect him and hold him in high regard. He always respected the anointing on my life to administrate and organize but was quick enough to realize the shift. When he invited me to speak for him during His Good Friday Service, it was a final confirmation of the calling for me to get involved with ministry in a capacity only God will show. I always felt I needed to start a Kingdom Community fellowship of some sort but was in a "holding pattern" for at least four years. When Dad, Dr. Tryon, introduced me on that Good Friday online service of April 2, 2021, as an apostle and acknowledged and recognized the gift as he did to me personally in the past, I accepted the challenge and responded to the call. It always takes a leader to recognize a leader. I feel greatly honored to have had my gift spotted, confirmed, and recognized by a man who understands the Kingdom and has sensed the calling of God on my life. Now that I have put my hand to the plow I can never look back.

Dr. Joseph Ripley was one of God's generals who identified a gift in me just after the departure of Dr. Munroe and even prayed for me when

I visited the Body of Christ Christian Church International Campus in 2015. Dr. Ripley demonstrated his confirmation of my ministry through his multiple invitations to his pulpit. He initially took a step of faith and took a risk by allowing me in his pulpit.

Ps. Roy and Rochel Oliveros, my friends in Davao, Philippines, are among those who acknowledged the gift of teaching in me and demonstrated it by their multiple invitations to participate in their ministries.

Dr. Dave and Mom Angie Burrows have been part of them who actively engaged me and told me I have a gift and ministry of teaching. Again, Dr. Dave is one of those who invited me multiple times and involved me in many ways.

I honestly believe that Dr. Myles would have expected me to live and teach what he taught me. See you in God's Vineyard!

A WORD TO THE
THIRD WORLD NATIONS

There are about 7.7 billion people who call planet earth their home and more than three quarters are identified as being part of Third World Nations. The term "Third World" is one that is despised and resented by many who interpret it to mean inferior, poor, underdeveloped, and to some degree, backwards.

An economist at the G-5 meeting in Geneva coined the term many years ago as an attempt to define the world in economic terms. The intent was not to degrade any group of people but rather to identify nations that fell within a common historical grid that resulted in their having common socioeconomic conditions and other similar characteristics.

In a nutshell, the term was an attempt to describe the grouping of people who were not allowed to develop or maximize their true potential as victims of colonial oppression and or regimes that suppressed and stifled progress of this group of people/the masses. These groups of people were not even allowed to benefit directly or indirectly from the benefits of the industrial revolution. They are found in all corners of the globe from every race, color, ethnic background, and nationality. Many of these people were used as slaves for the benefit of their oppressors and colonizers. Many of them have had their self-worth permanently destroyed.

The world-renowned leadership consultant, Dr. Myles Munroe, lived to correct this history and he was passionate about this people group. He poured his life into and invested a lot in teaching them how they could attain true freedom. While we cannot change history, we can correct it for the future of our children and grandchildren. It is now our turn to give hope to our world and shape the future.

I encourage you to live a life of purpose and serve your generation and the generations to come. Make yourself count in the struggle to bring freedom to our world. Hate oppression wherever you see it or are confronted with it. Serve your gift to the world – not as slaves to the colonizers and oppressors but as slaves to our callings and gifts. Always bear in mind that all humans were created in the image and likeness of God. Let us give all people of the world hope, dignity, and opportunities to fully become themselves. We came into the world for this very reason.

Do it for the oppressed; do it for the image of God – mankind.

END NOTES

Part 1

1. Bahamas Department of Civil Aviation, Air Accident Investigation and Prevention Unit, report number AAIPU# A14-005111, dated February 20, 2015.

Part 2

2. ChristianTT.com "Myles Munroe – Don't Be Afraid of Death"
3. commonwealth.org, "Commonwealth Heads of Government Meeting, Nassau, Bahamas. 16-22 October 1985"

Part 3

4. zachimalawi.blogspot.com/2012/10/dr-myles-munroe-greatest-revolutionary.html
5. www.kfm.co.ug/news/born-again-community-mourns-preacher-myles-monroe.html
6. standardmedia.co.ke, "Motivational Speaker Dr. Myles Munroe Who Spoke of His Death at JKL Show Dies"
7. mylesmunroeinternational.blogspot.com/2013/01/ghana-2012.html
8. Published: August 31, 2012 as posted by Dr. Myles Munroe on his Facebook page
9. https://www.gospelherald.com/articles/54348/20150211/late-christian-leader-myles-munroe-honored-by-israeli-government.html

Part 4

11. The Nassau Guardian Newspaper, dated 5/28/2014

ABOUT THE AUTHOR

Charlie Masala is a South African management consultant, speaker, and trainer. He
was personally mentored by the late leadership expert and Kingdom activist, Dr.
Myles Munroe. Charlie speaks on diverse
topics such as Leadership, Mentorship, Labor Relations, and Entrepreneurship.

As a Human Resources Generalist,
Charlie served corporate South Africa for
over twelve years before venturing out on his own as a Management
Consultant and Conference Speaker.

Charlie holds a National Diploma in Human Resources (Tshwane
University of Technology), Labor Relations Management Specialist
Certificate (IPM), and Certificates: Leading Change Program (Univer-
sity of Michigan Business School), Management Development Program
(University of Pretoria), and Thabo Mbeki African Leadership Program
(UNISA).

Charlie founded and served as Managing Director of Zoë Business
Consulting, National Director of Macedonia International Bible Fellowship (MIBF), Senior VP of International Third World Leaders Association (ITWLA), Board Member of The Myles and Ruth Munroe Foundation, and CEO of Myles Munroe International–Africa (Munroe Global).

Visit charliemasala.com or email: charliemasala@icloud.com.

www.ingramcontent.com/pod-product-compliance
Lightning Source LLC
Chambersburg PA
CBHW051811090426
42737CB00032B/2703